From The Deepest Darkness
To The Light of Hope

Jennifer Tracy

Copyright © 2021 Jennifer Tracy-Inspire, LLC
All rights reserved.

ISBN-13: 978-0-9993987-8-4
ISBN-10: 0-9993987-8-4

DEDICATION

This book is dedicated to my daughters,
McKayla Beth, Brittany Anne and Amber Lynn.
Of all the gifts and blessings in this life, you are the greatest.
I can honestly say I know and understand love because of you.

Statements of Support

~Such a well-written book. Not only a story of survival and triumph but a book that will help guide you through your own path as well. Jennifer Tracy speaks her truth in this book. It is an experiential workbook that will help many people. Not only those struggling with grief, depression, and thoughts of suicide but for all of us. Jennifer's heart is in this book and her mission is to see that it will give others hope. In my opinion, she attained that in this book. I highly recommend "From the Deepest Darkness to The Light of Hope."

—Robyn Spirtas, Ph.D LMFC

~As a long-time family doctor, I have born witness to oh-so-many patients with severe depression and suicidal thoughts. Convincing these folks that there is HOPE and there is a PATH back to joy has been one of the greatest challenges of my career. In the past, I felt I had to do it alone-just like my patients.

~Enter Jennifer Tracy. In "From the Deepest Darkness to The Light of Hope" Jennifer has laid bare the very essence of the pain those with severe depression and suicidal thoughts face. For those of us who haven't been deeply depressed, it's eye-opening and mind-blowing. For those in the grasp of depression her words read like an outstretched hand that says "Walk with me. You are not alone. I've walked this path and lived to tell the tale and you can too." Thus, I unreservedly recommend From the Deepest Darkness to The Light of Hope! It's a great read for anyone touched by suicide or deep depression. (And really, isn't that everyone?) It should be required reading for all medical residents during the psychiatry rotation. The more who read it the more lives will be saved!

—Anthony A. Doft, MD

~Having experienced "the fury" of depression and suicidal ideation, this book helped me find the words to describe some of what was going on in my head...Jennifer does a great job of balancing hope with the gritty reality of what she faced, and she helps you start to see your own story with some of that.

–Andrea Bowen - US Armed Forces

~This book is a must read for anyone who has ever struggled with depression and/or suicidal thoughts, or anyone who has a loved one with those issues who needs help and guidance. I know Jennifer personally, and her mission in life is to help people on their journey through the darkness so that they can engage into the light again. I think this book should be on every school library in the country. This is a very powerful book written by a brave and strong woman. Thank you for sharing your story, Jennifer.

–Denise Shuetter - Loving Mother

~This really is a book worth reading. From a male's perspective (like my own), the author's honesty and openness about her own life experience offers insight that will help most who are struggling with suicide, and those interested in learning about it, to understand how to navigate through the complexity of emotions and experiences that can be involved with it. Some of her examples, such as the check engine light analogy, makes sense in my mind. The resources and advice are worth considering as this is a subject often very personal and private. It really does offer hope and encouragement to live and reading the book made me appreciate my own life.

–Paul Erik -

~Jennifer's message saves lives… she's resilient and has overcome great odds.
—Chief Hernandez, Colorado State Patrol (Ret)

~Being a police officer, people think that we have great strength and courage to do our jobs. Real strength and courage is to move forward after tragedy and share your story so that others don't have to go through the same pain.
—Randy Carter, Weld County Sheriff

~I highly recommend Jennifer. Her message is powerfully inspiring in how to move forward in the wake of tragedy.
—Doug Erler, Director/Justice Services Department

~As a U.S. Veteran and career firefighter, I've been around friends and colleagues who have struggled with different "demons," even lost some…I myself struggled with diagnosed PTSD from issues relating to the job. I met Jennifer Tracy on LinkedIn and was impressed with the work she was doing for the "badge." She calls herself a civilian, but to me… she's as much a badge as anyone I have ever met. I thought I knew Jennifer Tracy well until I read her book and really just took in her story. I know tragedy, I've seen many of its faces, but Jennifer is just one of those rare people that took on more than any one person's share of grief…of pain and said no you won't beat me. I encourage everyone to read her story if anything to appreciate what you have. If you are one of those people that are struggling or have struggled out there, and there are many of us these days…then this should be required reading.

—Steven Straight, President/CCAI

CONTENTS

ACKNOWLEDGEMENTS

If you've ever written an acknowledgments section, then you know that it's overwhelming to think about everyone and everything it takes to accomplish any great work. I laugh a lot and say I am the combination of the 3,000 books I've read and the million songs I love. I thank God every day for my friends and family, you all have carried me through some of the darkest times of my life.

Thank you to those of you who have helped behind the scenes on this book. Dr. Shauna "Doc" Springer, I treasure your friendship, appreciate your guidance and wisdom during our professional collaborations and look forward to furthering our partnership on the Redefine Your Mission project and other future endeavors. Michael Sugrue, thank you for your support, friendship and for the way you fight for others through your powerful story. To my primary care physician, Dr. Doft, thank you for always providing a place for me to be honest and to get well. Your kindness and wisdom have been a large reason why I've been able to keep moving through the dark times of my life.

I also want to thank those friends who have been in my life the longest because you know me—the darkness and the light—and love me despite it. Micah and Jodie, thank you for walking through the fury of the storm with me and staying not only by my side but besides the girls as well. You both have stood by my side reassuring me that I was not alone in the darkness, thank you. Debra Ann, thank you for your friendship over the past twelve years; being your neighbor and friend was one of my greatest gifts in life. Paul, thank you for your undying friendship and support over the last eight years; your willingness to sacrifice and do great things without asking for anything in return is beyond comprehension. Brenda, thank you for your love and support over the last 24 years. I'm grateful to every one of my friends who have been in my life; I do genuinely wish I could write about how special each of you are to me. All my love to each of you.

As I think back on writing my first book in 2017 and now writing this book, it brings tears to my eyes to embrace the loss that we have been through as a family this past year. It's not possible to mention everyone in my family as each of you are weaved throughout my life. Mom, there is not a day that goes by that I don't miss you. I hold tight knowing you are with Brian and Brittany. I love you. I want to thank my grandparents for their undying love for all of us. Gram, you are terribly missed and our lives will never be the same without you. Dad, thank you for giving me life and for your love and support all of these years. I love you. Thank you to my step-mom Carol and to my step-dad Dave for the ways you both have played a part in who I am today as well; I love you both. To all of my grandparents, step-family, uncles, aunts, siblings, cousins, nieces and nephews, I love each and every one of you. Bob Peiffer, may your soul be at peace with all those who have gone before us. Shaune, please kiss my sweet Brittany, until we meet again I pray my life honors your service and sacrifice to our country.

Jeremy, your love and support both mean the world to me. You truly are my best friend and I look forward to another 30 plus years of adventure and love. Thank you also for your service to our country. I'm thankful I was able to meet your mom before she joined your father in heaven. I wish I could have met him as well. Through you I've been blessed to meet so many wonderful people that I now call friends and I'm thankful for their love and support.

Last but not least, McKayla and Amber, I love you. Being your mom has been the greatest joy and gift. You both mean the world to me. I know life has been hard, but together we've weathered the storms. Thank you for loving me. I'm so proud of the women you have both worked hard to become. Never stop believing in the power of your dreams and the power of your faith. I know your father and I taught you to have faith when you were young, but both of you helped restore my faith when the storms of life ran my soul dry. Amber, thank you for the thousands of hours we've spent on papers, workbooks and this book.

PREFACE

From the idea of this book until completion, *From the Deepest Darkness to The Light of Hope* has been the hardest thing I've done professionally. It is with the deepest respect that I have poured my heart out through these pages. If somehow you see yourself in this story, my hope is you will know beyond a shadow of a doubt, YOU ARE LOVED, you have **value** and **you** are worth any amount of fight it takes to save your life. Depression, anxiety, grief and any struggle with suicide can make you feel like you no longer have value. It changes all the rules. It doesn't discriminate. Suicide has touched rich and poor, young and old, those who believe in God and those who don't, famous and not, educated and uneducated, heroes and villains.

I designed this book to be an experiential workbook, packed with a lot of things to challenge the way you think. My hope is you will dig deep within yourself to find your own answers. You have a couple of options when reading this. You can read through it quickly and not take the time to answer the questions. However, no matter who you are, I recommend you take the time to really think about the questions at the end of each chapter and write out your answers. It is very powerful, I promise you. If you get stuck on a question, put the book down for awhile, fold the corner, but keep thinking about it and come back to it. If you disagree with what I am saying, write that down too. I'm ok with that.

I ask for your grace as you read this. Each of our stories are unique and woven together with their complexity. Please know, there is so much more to my story, I didn't write everything. This book is not so much about capturing all of the details as it is about courage, darkness, life, death, pain, hope, faith, choices and YOU.... It's about the deep-rooted passion I have to live life, never give up and to help others find the strength to do the same.

I truly believe, "someone else or something beyond my control may take my life now, but I however, WILL NOT!"

Please understand, no matter whether you yourself are struggling, know someone that is or have lost someone you love, reading this book may trigger intense emotions for you. It is not my intent to hurt you in any way, so if there is something said that upsets you, I apologize in advance. I would never want to hurt you. This is my personal story, what I've learned from it and what I did to survive. This book is not intended to take the place of seeing a therapist or physician.

If you are currently suicidal, it's recommended by therapists that you only read this book while being treated under the care of your primary care physician and/or licensed therapist. If you are struggling and need resources right away please reach out for help. It is a sign of great strength to get help. Again, please seek professional help if you are suicidal. I am alive today because of those trained professionals who've lovingly helped me survive the darkness and begin the journey back towards light and life.

All my best,

Jennifer Tracy

FOREWORD

When my mom first asked me to write the foreword for her book *From the Deepest Darkness to The Light of HOPE,* I knew it was something I wanted to do.

I would say that I have been very close to the issue of grief, depression, anxiety, and suicide. But truly, I think that right now, today, we all are.

I have lost acquaintances, classmates, teachers, and close family to suicide. I've seen people affected in every part of my life. Pain, trauma, and suicide hurt not only those who we've lost but also those of us who are left here as well. I think it is so important to keep talking about mental health and suicide. Many of the messages out there are very hurtful and unhelpful to those who are suffering or to those who have suffered. We need to pass on love, hope, and understanding not hate and/or judgment. More than anything, as someone who has struggled greatly with anxiety and grief after the loss of my father and sister, I want you to know there is HOPE.

I don't know many people who are willing to be transparent and vulnerable about their darkness and most painful struggles. Transparency is one thing you can count on in this book. Some of the darkest moments of my mom's life and some of the toughest in mine are shared in this book. We are both passionate about furthering our reach and hope the unmistakable honesty will light a fire in you. This is a book for everyone. If you interact with other people, then this book is for you.

There are many things that could be said about my mom. Somehow, she's always kept hope in sight when we encountered tragedy and hardship. She is full of wisdom and grace, and she has always put her whole heart into doing what she thought was best for herself and her two daughters, my sister, and me. Outside of our home, she has put hours and years into our community, schools, places of faith, First

Responders, veterans, and even with those who have found themselves in the correctional system.

There is no way to measure the positive ripple effect that started in Northern Colorado with her message of forgiveness, hope, and the power we have in our choice. Nothing has impacted my own life as much as growing up in a home where I knew I always had a place to communicate. I was free to share the thoughts and feelings I had regarding what I saw happening in my world—the world close to me and the one I was not close to in proximity. Things were not always right or well in our world, but I always knew there was a safe place to talk. I personally feel that many people do not grow up in an environment that promotes honest conversation, especially where there is conflict or disagreements. It is much easier for me to communicate about stress, frustration, and anxiety because of the way I grew up.

Healthy communication is one of my favorite topics! I hold these core beliefs about communication: Though not easy, it is always better to communicate than to hold in your feelings, we are always entitled to have our feelings, and what matters the most is the way we express them. It is okay to feel sad, angry, or any other emotion; however, we are always responsible for the way we react. I hope after reading this book you will believe in the importance of advocating for yourself in a healthy way.

The two chapters that I think have been written on my heart the most are "When Good Isn't Good Enough" (ch 5) and "Would You Take Insulin If Your Life Depended on It?" (ch 12). The mentality behind "When Good Isn't Good Enough" has really set the course for the way I view life and my role in it. I understand that, though I'm far from perfect, have made mistakes, and will still make mistakes, I am valuable and my life is worth living. The second chapter in this book that has impacted the way I view life the most is "Would You Take Insulin If Your Life Depended on It?"

Having heard this analogy many times over the years has made asking for help feel like second nature when I need it. I unknowingly saw what it looked like to face Stigma.

If I have something I'm struggling with, I'm going to look for answers, ask for help, and take the necessary actions towards the solution or solutions. I know this requires courage, but with practice, it has become easier.

I would hope that through reading this book, you would find even one thing to hold on to, to make your everyday life better, and lead you on to a successful journey through a life lived with strong mental health, love for yourself, others, and God.

Amber Lynn is a Colorado native. Her purpose and passion collide as she serves others and spreads joy like glitter. She has been writing songs for 12 years. She is the co-author of Shatter The Strongholds, a prayer journal and workbook. Amber loves to travel, enjoys the outdoors, to learn about different cultures and also find new ways to make an impact in her corner of the world.

Chapter One

Victories on The Hill

If there was one thing I could share with the world in regard to depression, anxiety, grief, PTSD and thoughts of suicide, it would be that everyone comes to that place of pain, despair, darkness; that ledge, so very differently.

After all these years of navigating this very complex battle myself, speaking and working with clients, what I've come to realize is this: because there is not a one-size-fits-all solution to win a mental health battle, there are a lot of hurtful, confusing messages out there. There are a lot of good-hearted people who believe that what worked for them will also work for others. These people at times stand on a hill waving a flag proclaiming, "look, the answer to what you are facing, it's over here. It worked for me, so it should work for you too."

The most powerful and profound lesson I feel I can teach you is, if you want to win the battle you are facing, be it grief, depression, anxiety, PTSD or even thoughts of suicide, you must decide that you want to know everything you can about it. Be open minded, stop being stubborn.

As you go through this book, take what you need. If something that I say resonates with you, write it down. Research it. Write out what your plan of action will be. Use the worksheets from that section. If something I say bothers you. Write that down. Ask yourself, why?

I'd like to give you a few examples of real individuals with Victories On The Hill. To preserve confidentiality, these names are fictional and are for teaching purposes only. However, the situations themselves are real as I have personally witnessed every one of them happen in the lives of my clients and others I've known.

Suzy, who was born with bi-polar mood patterns, has struggled for 20 years with depression, mood swings, self-harm, anxiety and sometimes thoughts of suicide.

Recently, she heard Joe waving his flag from the hill of victory saying that western medications were killing people, and that the key to relief from depression, anxiety and mood swings is meditation, working out and a drastic change in diet, since this is what has changed his life.

Maybe in reading this you can see very clearly here that this is akin to the oft-used expression of comparing apples to oranges.

You see, Joe doesn't have bi-polar. No thyroid issues. He doesn't struggle with addiction. He is very successful yet he has struggled deeply with depression, anxiety and mood swings.

The message that Joe proclaims from his hill of victory can be very confusing to Suzy and could even potentially do more harm than good.

It took Suzy many years to first accept she needed to take medication for her bi-polar mood symptoms. She thoroughly researched her condition and now, with the help of a team of trusted individuals, including her Rabbi, therapist, and husband has successfully managed it for years. For Suzy, medication has been life-changing in the best possible way.

While Joe's victory is powerful and his willingness to share his story to help others is admirable, delivering his message in a black and white manner without regard to context, or considering the differences in circumstances, can be hurtful to others who may actually need to include medication in their personal wellness plan.

This is a second example.

After many years of struggling with anxiety, people pleasing, self-condemnation and addiction, Judy, a devout Christian, found total life change for herself through a program and group called "Celebrate Recovery." She found a large community of people just like herself who were struggling. They met weekly, sometimes twice a week, in group format, to encourage, support, and pray for each other. These people in her life became integral for her sustained victory because community was very important to her and so was praying and reading the Bible.

Judy never took medication, has been sober now for 8 years and is thriving in life. Such a victory.

Sadly, on Judy's hill of victory though, she believes that everyone can find this same freedom and victory by joining a "Celebrate Recovery" group at church, where they can get involved and do life with other people. She truly believes that people can pray through anything they are facing, especially if they have an accountability partner and go to church.

Again, Judy is a fictitious name – but this story is one that I personally have seen way too many people experience.

While Judy's freedom from addiction, anxiety, and self-condemnation came from practicing her Christain beliefs or spiritual beliefs, staying in the community, and having accountability in her life; her message that prayer and community are the keys to recovery is problematic. She may deliver this message repeatedly to many people, showing full confidence and unwavering faith in this perceived solution.

When this message is delivered without regard to the individual circumstances at play, this can be hurtful to others. It may even increase stigma for those who find that including various other treatments such as EMDR (Eye Movement Desensitization and Reprocessing) and/or CBT (Cognitive Behavior Therapy) medication, Yoga, horse or equine therapy, and meditation, etc. are essential for their personal wellness practice.

Here is an additional story. True story, fictitious name.

While this is a touchy subject to talk about, I feel it's important. I once had a client, let's say his name was Joey. Joey was as healthy as they come. Joey married his high school sweetheart. They had three beautiful children and he pursued his lifelong passion, to serve as a Police Officer. Through hard work and perseverance, he had risen all the way to Police Chief and held that role for 16 years.

After their children were born, things on the home front with his wife were very strained. Things unraveled further as he poured himself into his career and her focus was on raising the children. Their communication issues led them to drift apart. He tried to protect her from the things he saw at work by bottling them up. She couldn't stand his dark humor or how distant he had become. Joey never thought he would ever be 'that guy' that would cheat on his wife, but it happened. Joey had an affair with a nurse and this went on for about 4 weeks. Then Joey ended the affair. He never told anyone. He stayed married and by the time he became my client, he was battling severe depression, nightmares, flashbacks, sleeplessness and thoughts of suicide.

Again, it may seem so obvious to you that trying to compare Joey's story to Judy's or Suzy's would be ridiculous, right? Yet, so often this is exactly what happens - sometimes by society in general, and sometimes by mental health professionals.

When Joey went in for his annual physical, the one that would be stored in his file at work, his doctor asked how things were going. Joey said he was struggling with sleep and was irritable all the time. His doctor suggested he try some medication but Joey feared losing his job if someone found out, so he declined. Clearly, Joey was struggling deeply with symptoms his doctor could treat, yet, Joey also broke a moral code that no-one knew about.

How can we expect our primary care physicians to know the complexity of how we should treat and help those who are struggling, such as our first responders and veterans - the pressures they face and the stigma that may be part of seeking help for their struggles? Is it fair to think that our primary care physician would know to ask us if we've had an affair, if someone in our lives had just passed away or if we feared sharing the truth with them? These deeper wounds can make it hard for professionals to help us if they don't know everything that has happened.

I'm not pointing fingers at our healthcare professionals, rather trying to make a point that either we, as individuals, need to learn how to advocate for ourselves, or we need to help our professionals see that they are a part of the big picture.

Working one to one with Joey as a client was rewarding. I'm happy to share with you that when we started working together, we did 3 to 4 quick self-assessments and he rated his own level of depression, shame, irritability, sleeplessness and thoughts of suicide. We put a plan together to work on each of those issues independently and look at them holistically. This included bringing in other professionals. I share this with you to make a very clear point. One, no amount of medication could help Joey work through the shame and guilt he felt. Two, we had to work around social stigma to help him solve his struggles with insomnia and make sure he didn't lose his job in the meantime.

Do you see how every one of these stories needed its unique solution? So many have found life on the other side of these battles. Sadly, often when we are in the middle of our personal battles, we can't see this. I hope that by the end of this book, you will discover insights to apply in your own life.

Reflection

My deepest desire with this book is to go on a journey with you. I want you to walk down each hall, open each door, see the darkness, light and stay as long as you need until you figure out —where do you see yourself in my story. What applies to you? What actions do you need to take?

Before you begin, it's important that you map out for yourself- Where you are? Why are you reading this? What are you hoping to get from it? And then, really answer the questions at the end of each chapter.

To complement this, I have put together a journal and self-assessment section in the back of this book. This is just a starting place.

If you want to win the battle you are facing, you must decide that no matter what, you want to grow. The concept of 'Let Your Diagnosis Be Your Roadmap To Recovery' is something you will hear me talk about in my **online course- Win The Mental Health Battle You Are Facing**. In this course I guide you through the content in this book, plus much more. Make a commitment to yourself today that you will not let a diagnosis define you, rather use it to understand what obstacles and barriers you will need to overcome and/or manage.

If you deal with ongoing stress and trauma, are a First Responder, work in emergency services, are a Veteran or love and support those who are, Doc Shauna Springer and I have put together an online "Tactical Toolkit" where we combined some of our greatest work (including my online course) to help you navigate the <u>unique</u> battle you are facing. Find both of these resources at www.redefineyourmission.com.

I'm ready to share with you the journey I've forged to find my personal "Victory on The Hill." Are you ready? Let's Go!

Questions

What is something you are working to overcome? Where do you feel stuck?

_____

_____

_____

_____

Can you pinpoint when this started?

_____

_____

_____

What have you tried? What has worked? What has not worked?

_____

_____

_____

_____

Use the worksheets in the back of this book to help guide you through these chapters or grab my online course for an in-depth guided experience. www.jennifertracy-inspire.com/books

Chapter Two

What I Learned from Psychology 101 at Age 19

As a freshman at Metropolitan State College, I was given the assignment to write a paper on nature versus nurture.

My paper discussed how I felt it was both. I believed then and still do that we are born with a certain set of DNA, yet, I had already seen by the age of 19 that our environments definitely shape who we are.

Some of my earliest childhood memories that stem from environmental influence are difficult to relive. Here is one.

Both my older brother Jeff and I were victims of sexual assault by someone outside of our family. It's hard to comprehend the magnitude of what really happened during what should have been an innocent game of hide and seek. I was robbed of something that I would never be able to get back. When we got home that night from our family friends house, I remember hiding under my bed. When my mom came in to tuck me in, she asked me why I was hiding. I never spoke about what really happened until years later in therapy.

Sadly, my brother turned to drugs as a coping mechanism. One day he stole a motorcycle and crashed, going 120 mph. The image of him lying in a hospital bed hooked up to machines is something I will never be able to erase. He was in a coma for several months and eventually recovered. As part of his recovery, he had to learn how to walk again. He has lived with that TBI (Traumatic Brain Injury) his entire life.

Nature vs. Nurture

I love my brother so much. I wish we could go back to simpler days of playing Atari games, go-karts, and jumping on the trampoline. All of this happened the same year my parents divorced. Watching my brother go through all of this was devastating. **I promised myself that I would never do drugs.** I had no idea how hard it would be to keep this promise.

For a short time, my dad remarried his second wife. I then went from being the youngest to being the middle child when my half-brother Brandon was born. Having Brandon as a little brother taught me so much, plus he was fun to babysit as a teenager.

Another promise I made was when I grew up and became a mom, I vowed that I would protect my children from abuse, divorce, drugs, all of that. **I unknowingly felt like I had to be perfect. I loved everyone but myself. Somewhere buried in the trauma was a driven woman who hid the need to be perfect behind the dark side of resilience.**

I didn't realize it then, but because of that trauma I made deep rooted commitments and agreements with myself, some of which have taken decades to heal.

Even though my childhood was tough, I have so many happy memories too. I was very outgoing and had a lot of friends. One memory that I have with my dad that I will always cherish was balancing on his feet as he laid on his back. I was learning gymnastics and his feet seemed like the perfect place to practice balancing. My mom was very active in my life. She took me to Girl Scouts, gymnastics, and sometimes church. She was the first person I remember reading the Bible with. Back in the '80s, we were allowed to play outside, run around with our friends and hang out until it was dark. Both of my parents loved music, and I have always shared this same passion. It's impossible to hear Frank Sinatra and not think of my dad. To say that my dad loved Sinatra's music would be an understatement.

Life was not easy for my dad when he was young, and sadly, the abuse he suffered at the hands of his father had a lasting impact. It breaks my heart thinking about the things he endured. What I feel the most when I think about my dad is that he is incredibly kind, skilled with his hands, and his love for our family has always been evident to me. My parents had very similar childhoods. My mom's was equally traumatic.

Even though I would describe my mom as what I would call a "people-pleaser," she was very genuine, compassionate, and giving. My mom always put others ahead of herself. Her love and support of me never wavered.

During that same year of college, I took a required public speaking class. The first speech I gave was on alcoholism, something very close to my heart and personal life. Again, I had already witnessed its effects and watched as it deeply affected my family. I still have the paper I wrote from that class with the professor's handwritten note attached to it. That speech included fond memories that I wrote about my dad.

I love my dad. If I'm honest, I know that I get my strong will from him, which unites us. It's almost as if writing that paper and giving that speech somehow thrust me into a battle to test me on how much we genuinely are shaped by the environment vs. our DNA.

For as long as I can remember, my dad has been married to Carol, my step-mom. My dad's marriage to Carol brought my sister Kim and brother Shaune into my life. Carol is a remarkable woman, quiet, sweet in nature, and tough as nails. Sometime after my parents divorced, my mom went out country dancing with her friends and ran into her high school sweetheart David. Though they never technically married, I've always called him my step-dad, even when he didn't want me to. AND with that- David brought the entire Keberlein family into my life. Throughout my teenage years, I know I tested David's patience. I'll never forget the robust conversations and debates we had about faith and God. David taught me to drive, starting first with the tractor and then a six-speed. Outside of Carol and David, my grandma Phyllis and grandpa, or "Poppy," as I like to call him, have instilled so many rich family traditions in me and have always been a significant source of strength. One thing I have never lacked was family. I come from a long line of warriors. My family is rich in diversity, love, and a whole lot of imperfections.

As you can see, I had plenty of nature and nurture to shape who I was.

I remember thinking at age 19 that I had my head on right despite everything that I had been through. Academically, I was at the top of my class, graduated a year early from high school and earned my cosmetology license at the same time. By the age of 24, I was married with three beautiful daughters, owned a home and had a small hair salon. The girls' dad, Brian, and I had met while country-western dancing at the Grizzly Rose in Denver when we were 18. Neither of us planned to have children so young, but I can say confidently we would not have made a different choice when it came to jumping into being parents of twins at 20. We both had identical twin cousins. We were really excited to be a family.

Brian's upbringing was very similar to mine, with one key difference; his mother was hateful towards Brain's biological father Bob because he wrestled with alcohol addiction. It's not my intention to disrespect Brian's mom; however, this stark difference of how she treated those struggling is essential for you to know as I share the rest of my story.

I'm not going to lie to you. Our life together was filled with strain. Our twin daughters were born 7 weeks early at, 2lbs 13oz and 3lbs 10oz. My pregnancy with them was a fight to save their lives. They had a syndrome called Twin to Twin Transfusion. One of our twin daughters, Brittany was born with Cerebral Palsy, and as I said earlier, we had three girls by the time we were 24. We both came from broken homes, and from the beginning we said "Divorce was not an option."

Me and Brian when our twins were 5 days old.

Throughout our marriage, Brian wrestled deeply to control his anger. I've always felt as though his mom made him choose between her or me. This added an insane amount of stress to our relationship. There is no doubt that his mom and I were unmistakably different. All I ever really wanted was her love and approval. She was incredibly talented when it came to flower arrangements. Though she may not realize it, I learned from watching her and give credit to her for the arrangements I've made for my daughters and family throughout the years.

Something that comes naturally for me is to be open and honest. I can remember several occasions where being honest in front of Brian's mom was followed by her comment, "you shouldn't talk about those things." I'd wager a bet there was hidden pain under her words; She never talked about her past or childhood. Despite what she thought, I didn't let her view of what I should and should not speak about sway me. I'll never forget this moment with Brian in line outside on the campus of UNC. As we stood there, I found myself talking to the ladies in front of us. Brian's words still bring a smile to my face; he said, "I swear you have a sign on your forehead that says— "say hi to me." He would tease me about this for years to come. I'm pretty sure the sign is still there.

Me and my twins in 1995.

I never dabbled in substance abuse, and I thought I had done everything right. While I was proud of breaking negative patterns I had seen in my family, I struggled with self-defeating behaviors. I found myself facing circumstances with the odds stacked against me. Despite all of this, we loved each other. Brian had a deep passion for sports. Dan Marino with the Miami Dolphins and CU Boulder college football were a regular on our tv each week.

Both of us shared a love for music. He called me "JT" and always wanted me to publish a music cd with the music he had written. As a wedding gift, my dad and Carol gifted us a trip to Nashville for our honeymoon. A fun excursion we enjoyed while there was an evening dinner cruise. I had no idea that part of the night was karaoke. Back then, it took a lot of courage for me to sing "Is there life out there" by Reba McEntire. Who can match Reba? She is still one of my favorite singers. I didn't get any offers to record a music cd, but the fun we had will always remain with me.

When we first met, Brain said he didn't believe in God and had no interest in going to church. However, when things became very rocky in our marriage, it was in a small Christian Church called Northern Hills where we found something we had not yet experienced together. Faith. Something bigger than us that we deeply believed "loved us." One thing that was refreshing about this church was the way they genuinely connected with those who attended. In fact, the first sermon we heard was on relationships and the assistant pastor's wife, Carol Ann sang "You don't bring me flowers… anymore" by Neil Diamond. Their teaching style was just what we needed- real people talking about real struggles. Our new community brought friends and events to keep us busy. Some of these friendships have carried me to this day. Jodie, thank you for walking through the Fury with me all these years.

Our youngest daughter Amber's birth. February 1998

I'll never forget the heart change in Brian over the years to follow. Though he wrestled with his demons, he was also bold about his faith. The year he wrote his father Bob a letter sharing his own story of finding forgiveness and then extending that same love to him was remarkable. I wish that Brian's encounter with forgiveness was enough to erase all the years of pain and anger he brought into our marriage, but that's not the case. After all these years, what I've come to realize is that forgiveness is much like a relationship- It has a start date, and it takes a commitment to keep it alive and active. Relationships are tough, especially when two people bring in so much past baggage. I brought my fair share.

I've designed this book to be raw, real and full of strategies to help you win whatever battle you are facing. Depression, anxiety, PTSD and thoughts of suicide can make us feel powerless. Take control of your life and Take Your Power Back!

Something I've been teaching now for 12 years is how, at any given moment, you can stop and use the strategy I'm about to share to help you focus. Some people call this mindfulness. Twenty years ago, when I was in a psychiatric unit (more on that as my story unfolds), they taught us to live in the "here and now." Whatever you want to call it, it's a technique to train your mind.

No matter what situation you are facing, stop and see if it is one of the five things on the next page. I use this technique every single day. It's like breathing for me. This technique can help you quickly stop and switch your focus away from things you can't control or change- to the one thing that you ALWAYS can- YOU!

No matter what is going on, you always have the power to choose what you want to do, how you want to respond, or what actions you want to take to grow.

There are FIVE things
that we have no power to control or change.
Knowing these things can help you
focus on what you can change.

TIME/DEATH...
We all will face death— it's a part of life!
DNA...
No one gets to pick the DNA we have!
WEATHER...
While we can be more prepared for natural disasters
we can't control them from happening!
THE PAST...
No one can go back and change things done to us or what we did!
OTHER PEOPLE/THEIR CHOICES
We can do our best to influence others but
ultimately change is up to them!

Reflections:

Every one of us is born to a set of parents we didn't choose. We don't get to pick the color of our skin or the DNA we are born with. We don't have the power to control whether or not our parents are good to us or choose to be active in our lives. We do however get to decide what we are going to do about that. Isn't it interesting how children can grow up in the same home and go on to live two completely different lives? Though not easy, if you keep your focus on what you can change, instead of what you can't, it's empowering. What do you think?

Questions:

Is your life set in place by the DNA you were born with or by the environment you grew up in?

_____

_____

_____

What was your life like growing up?

_____

_____

_____

What is something that YOU currently have the power to change?

_____

_____

_____

Chapter Three

The Dark Maze

My story with depression started in 1999. I was 24 years old and now had three daughters, twins almost five and a one-year-old. At that time, I had to have a complete hysterectomy. I had endometriosis really bad and it was everywhere. While I'm sure that many women would love to not have their monthly cycle or periods anymore, having to have a "complete" hysterectomy was not something to look forward to at such a young age. A partial hysterectomy would have left my ovaries, one of the estrogen hormone-producing and regulating organs in a woman's body.

After the surgery, I started having symptoms of depression, something I had never experienced before. Things I used to be able to do seemed impossible to accomplish. It felt like I had an elephant on my shoulders. I found myself withdrawing from my friends and family, and when I did go to functions, I felt numb and distant. My sleeping patterns changed. I wasn't sleeping well, and I remember feeling irritable. There was a constant battle between how I acted and what was really going on inside of my mind. When my daughters would accidentally spill the milk, inside I was very agitated, and I remember wanting to yell at them, but I worked hard to still respond reasonably. It wasn't like that every day, but as time went on, it got worse. I constantly felt like I was at war with the thoughts inside of my own mind.

For over a year, I continued fighting my silent battle. I tried a few times to tell Brian how I felt, but he seemed to have no understanding about what I was going through or what he could do to help me. I felt so alone. I remember journaling a lot to get my feelings out, and it helped.

These journals have helped me in times of confusion to remember what was going on and how far I have come. During one of my follow-up appointments with my doctor, I expressed how I was crying a lot, couldn't sleep and felt agitated all of the time. I was given a survey with questions to answer to see if I had symptoms of depression. My doctor suggested I take an antidepressant. I remember feeling strong displeasure in response, so I left and went home to explore my other options. For me, medication felt like I was taking something that would alter my mind or control me.

For several months following, I met with a homeopathic consultant who gave me natural remedies to help with depression, including St. John's Wart, Gingko Biloba and 5-HTP (Hydroxytryptophan). I found no relief from taking these. At the time, I considered natural remedies as an option that would help my body heal itself rather than something that altered me. I know many people who take natural remedies for all types of ailments and they work. From what I've learned, it tends to take longer to build up in your system, thus requiring longer time periods to start working. I don't know why they work for some and not others. Again, we all have to find what works for us.

During this time, I remember "believing" God could heal me and that if I had enough faith, I could get out of this dark maze in which I was trapped. As the days went on, the guilt and shame continued to get worse. With no relief from the natural products I was taking, I finally gave in and tried an antidepressant called Prozac. While I did feel a bit better, the **guilt of having to take medication** was overwhelming. I felt like I was letting myself down by taking the medicine. Up until this point, depression remained a constant struggle, but I had no thoughts of suicide. I just felt hopeless, tired of fighting and constantly like I was letting down my family and daughters. Every day I found myself preparing for mental warfare. I spent every ounce of my being taking care of my daughters and my household duties.

Looking back now, it's hard to imagine that *that* dark got darker.

Reflections:

I believe my battle with depression started because of my hysterectomy and the lack of estrogen in my body. However, I know enough now that previous trauma added an emotional piece to this battle. A lot of what kept me stuck in "The Dark Maze" was misguided, deep-rooted beliefs and commitments I'd made with myself as a survivor of childhood abuse. I realize now that I had never worked through the sexual abuse from my childhood, which led to extreme shame and guilt. Also, I was addicted to being perfect and didn't even know it.

Questions:

If you or someone you know has struggled with depression, can you pinpoint when it started? Was there something physical or an event that triggered it? Do you know why you are depressed?

_____

_____

_____

Can you relate to the feeling of doing everything that you possibly can to help yourself, yet still finding no relief?

_____

_____

_____

When I shared that I felt guilty about taking medication, did you find yourself relating to this or asking yourself why I would feel guilt and shame about a doctor's recommendation? I wish someone had asked me then, "Jennifer, why do you feel ashamed right now? Why do you have such a strong opposition to taking medication?"

_____

_____

_____

Do you recognize any deep-rooted beliefs or commitments you have made with yourself that have kept you from moving forward in life? This can be about medication, the need to be perfect or never challenging the negative mind talk that says you are less than perfect.

_____

_____

_____

I wish I'd been able to see that unhealthy people in my current environment continued to add to the shame, guilt and pain I was experiencing. This is important to recognize. While you may not be able to change your environment overnight, knowing that it is toxic or unhealthy can help you understand what's going on. What does your current environment look like?

_____

_____

_____

Have you ever journaled? Did it help?

Your thoughts…

_____
_____
_____
_____
_____
_____
_____
_____
_____
_____
_____
_____
_____
_____
_____
_____
_____
_____
_____
_____
_____

Chapter Four

The Fury

The first time I had the thought to kill myself, I was scared beyond belief. I had been struggling for quite a while with depression. I also was seeing a therapist every week. I learned during a therapy session the difference between having thoughts of suicide and actually planning it. I remember becoming hyper-vigilant about keeping an eye on myself. I didn't understand then how someone could make a plan without anyone knowing about it. I didn't want to hurt myself, but my thoughts constantly told me I did. My mind just kept saying, "It will never end," "It's hopeless," "Just do it," and "Your kids are better off without you."

I began to reach out to people who I thought I could trust. I had a couple of friends who were depressed as well and were taking medications. I opened up to my pastor and his wife, and they were kind and prayed with me. Their prayers, however, did not change the dark maze I was in, nor help me out. Their love did help me to not feel alone.

I continued to feel like I was trapped in some kind of maze where there was no escape. It seemed like friends disappeared, and the guilt, shame and pain continued to grow. I was getting three to four hours of sleep at night and wasn't hungry half of the time. I can still hear my mother in law say, "You're so thin. Do you have an eating disorder?" As you can imagine, that only added to my shame. I was doing everything I possibly could to survive another day. I took medicine, saw a therapist, took care of my daughters, and did my best to sleep and keep up with everything. It was messy. During this time, my mom was there in the midst, helping in every way. As I shared, she was always putting others ahead of herself.

As I came close to the two-year mark of struggling with depression and thoughts of suicide, my body began to completely break down. The three to four hours of sleep became less. I struggled to stay asleep most nights. I had very little of an appetite and felt weak and exhausted. Instead of anger, I just felt numb. It was a struggle to even shower. I put all the energy I did have into taking care of my children and my home. I made sure they were fed and bathed and that their clothes were clean and their homework was done. Bedtime stories, Disney movies and coloring became our favorite things.

**This was me when I was battling my two year struggle with suicide.
(In this picture is my daughter Amber and our kitty Halley.)**

By this point, I was no longer working. Financial hardship was an everyday struggle. I was still taking my medication and seeing a therapist. I believed the lie that I was less of a mother and woman because of what I was experiencing. I also started to believe my daughters were better off without me. I couldn't stand the person inside my mind or the woman in the mirror. I had to work hard every minute of every day to be who I wanted to be. When people said things to me like, "Think of your daughters. How can you even think about taking your life?" This only made me feel worse. I remember thinking, I am thinking of them. I'm broken. I'm a burden. They are better off without me.

> I remember thinking, I am thinking of them. I'm broken. They are better off without me.

As the friends begin to leave, you think, "See, there is something wrong with me." As the mean people in your life continue to judge you and point fingers, you start to break down. Every little look of judgment cut deep.

Despite the struggle, I somehow found a way to go on every day until the moment my mind crossed over from hurting just me to somehow hurting my children, and then I was done.

The day my thoughts of suicide took a turn toward actually attempting suicide was the day that I had to make the bravest decision I would have to face as a 26-year-old mother of three. This day will be burned in my mind forever.

"Did that thought really just go through my mind? Oh my God… no… not my children."

I had picked my daughters up from school and they were fighting in the backseat of our minivan. Then the most horrifying thought went through my mind. "Jennifer, just stop this pain now, drive as fast as you can and drive into a wall." I almost threw up in my minivan. Flashbacks of friends and family members who had taken their lives ran through my mind. I had seen and experienced the aftermath of others committing suicide. I also remembered the news coverage of those who not only took their own lives but harmed others as well. I remember at the time not understanding how someone could do that. All I can do is speak for myself. During that challenging time in my life, it felt like my mind had been kidnapped and held for ransom. **What would it take to get my mind back?**

> During that challenging time
> in my life, it felt like
> my mind had been
> kidnapped and
> held for ransom.

After regaining my thoughts, I drove straight home. I got the girls out of the van and told them to go up to their rooms and find toys to play with until Daddy got home. I told them to stay in their rooms, no questions asked. I remember my hands trembling as I picked up the phone to call my husband. He answered, and I just said, "You need to get home now." He tried asking questions, and I just said, "Please, come home now."

When Brian got there, I told him I could no longer fight this fight. I had tried everything, and I had just had the most horrific thought and I was no longer safe to mother my own children. I asked him to find someone to watch the girls and to take me to the hospital.

I had been to the emergency room plenty of times before, but never for this. I was almost frozen numb when the man at the front desk asked me, "How can I help you, Ma'am?"

I said, "I'm really sick, and I need help."

He said, "What's wrong with you?"

I just stood there.

What was wrong with me? I started to cry, and I said, "I'm having thoughts of killing myself," and "I don't know what to do."

I was going to end my life that day for many reasons, but I know for sure that one of those reasons was—I was tired of fighting the many thoughts that waged war in my mind.

He said, "Stay right here, Ma'am, I'll be right back." He came out with another man, and right away they took me into your typical ER room. Some ER rooms are only separated by a sheet; this room was three walls and a glass door. I was thankful no one would be able to hear me share what I had to say. It wasn't long before someone came in and started to talk to me. I did my best to tell him the whole story: the surgery, the medications I was on, the therapist I was seeing, how tired I was and how long I'd been fighting this fight. Not long after that, I was put into an ambulance and taken to the psychiatric unit. I had never been to one before, and I knew nothing about the rules. I had no idea I had just chosen "Prison."

During this time, Brian was faithful and did his best. Sadly he was working in sales, and once I stopped working in my hair salon, our income dropped by thousands of dollars a month, and he was earning little to no income at all. I can see it now clear as day. He was stuck. Back then, it felt like he wasn't even there. I wanted a warrior to come in and save the day. The truth is, we both needed help and resources.

If you're reading this and you've been in a psychiatric unit or know someone who has, then you know that it really is like prison, a prison designed to keep you safe from yourself and others. No silverware. No way out.… I wish there were advocates who prepared you for such an event.

Why did I feel like a criminal? Why did I feel ashamed and worthless? This feeling of shame and guilt helps me understand why so many choose not to get help. These feelings make you want to isolate yourself. I know that so many people don't have a good experience in the psychiatric unit; not all psychiatric units are the same. They aren't a magic pill. No matter what though, it's up to you to try and see the purpose of that place. If you have been there, you are alive reading this. That is so powerful. Your story isn't over yet. Please don't give up.

This picture reminds me of the psychiatric unit where I stayed.

I only wish I could bottle up courage and hope and share it with those struggling because that decision to get help saved my life. I'm alive today to see the most beautiful events in my life because I was kept safe from myself.

> I only wish I could bottle up courage and hope and share it with

There really are no words to describe the emotions I feel every time my daughters reach new milestones in their own lives: birthdays, high school graduations and even my oldest daughter graduating from The University of Northern Colorado. For myself, I never would have returned to college, created community programs or lived daringly by cliff diving in Glendo, Wyoming. As hard as it is to comprehend, you wouldn't be reading this if I had lost my fight with depression and suicide. I am humbled writing this, I know many, too many, have lost their battle.

Again, up until this point in my struggle, I had not once hurt myself or anyone else. I had done everything I possibly could to help myself. I thought I had done the right thing. **Would the psychiatric unit help me?**

The first thing that happened in the psychiatric unit was the doctor had labs drawn and ran some diagnostic tests. I was mandated to participate in the daily activities and to attend group therapy. When the blood work came back, my doctor informed me I had thyroid disease and no estrogen in my body. I was relieved yet puzzled. None of my previous doctors had run tests, and I didn't know it was possible to check your estrogen levels. I had been taking estrogen since my hysterectomy, so I had assumed it was doing the job of my ovaries. The doctor started me on a very high dose of an antidepressant called Effexor and a medication to help me sleep at night.

I remember in the evening of the second night, we had to watch a movie called "The Joy of Laughing," and at one point, we had to grab our fat rolls and turn to the person next to us and wiggle them. I was furious at the lady who made us watch this. I kept thinking, **"I'm struggling with taking my life, something very serious, and you want me to grab my fat rolls and laugh about it."**

I wouldn't accept phone calls from anyone except my husband. After several days passed, my daughters came up to visit me. They thought I was in the hospital. Eventually, my Mom, Dad, Carol, Dave, Uncle Bob and Grandparents came up to visit me, too. This was the first time in my life I felt strong emotions that seemed to conflict with each other. I was happy my family loved me, was there for me and that I wasn't alone, yet I felt such shame. I wanted to be alone and truly wanted to hide under a rock.

Within days of sleeping, I had more physical energy than I had in the previous two years. It no longer felt like I had an elephant sitting on my shoulders every time I went to move. That place and those moments represented the lowest time of my life. I've never felt as much personal shame, and guilt as I did then. I believed I had failed. Somehow, I felt it was my fault that I was there, and I couldn't bear to speak to anyone.

I can tell you that still, even at this point, I wanted to live. I wanted to get back to me. I wanted so desperately to stop feeling the way I did. And I wonder, even though I may never know the answer, do people who take their own lives really ever, on a deep level, want to die? Or is there something else they really want? To be understood, to find joy and peace again, to find love or to stop hurting all of the time? To stop their mind from telling them the lies that it demands are true?

> And I wonder, even though I may never know the answer, do people who take their own lives really ever, on a deep level, want to die?

As I write about that time in my life, I feel sad yet have a great deal of acceptance and peace. I would not wish these experiences on anyone, not the suicidal thoughts, loss, or trauma. Despite my struggles and brokenness, I can say confidently that it is **"Better to Be than to Not Be at All."** It is better to be this version of me than to have left my children and family in that way. The path it took to get here was, in fact, a journey. Change in every area of my life did not happen overnight. Even still, I have things I'm working to change in my own life. Despite my struggles, I talk about the darkness because it takes away the power that it has over me & hopefully you.

I call suicide "The Fury" because it is very complex. It's crucial when you are struggling with depression, anxiety, and thoughts of suicide that you find a team of people to help you. It's important to embrace how complex of an issue this is. Don't give up until you find the people that get you. They are out there.

The suicidal mind is convincing. It feeds shame, guilt, fear & hopelessness. Please don't believe the lie that says it will never get better. The lie that says you are a burden. I know it can feel like a no win situation for those of us fighting. This stigma doesn't stop even after you have sought treatment. I get it.

This has to stop! We can not tell people to seek help and then punish them when they do. If you have gone to seek help—I hope you know how courageous that is. Stand in that. That's powerful and no-one can take that from you. I'm proud of you.

More often than not, going to any type of specialized treatment is looked on as a last resort option. As you continue with me on my journey, you'll see why I can empathize with those who struggle to reach out. I truly understand the real fear of losing everything if you reach out.

Take a moment with me if you will, and just pause. What is your truth, your story? I know as I write this that YOU have a story and something has compelled you to read this. If you have lost someone to suicide please know that I am so sorry. If you have battled or currently are battling the "The Fury" I'm sorry. No matter who you are I am honored that you have chosen to read my story. You are not alone.

Reflections:

At the end of the day, it's hard to accept that suicide and thoughts of suicide start in the mind. How do we win a battle in an unseen arena? Recall with me the battle I had with my thoughts: "It will never end," "It's hopeless," "Just do it," and "Your kids are better off without you." Thoughts are interesting, aren't they? I never asked for the horrific thoughts that played on repeat all day long. Yet, I felt responsible for them and, after time, I started to believe the thoughts. This is true for any negative thought that we give permission to stay. Has that ever occurred to you? That we gradually believe the thoughts and lies that we are unaware of or don't fight? Solving my own struggle with suicide took some time. Remember, I discovered that I had thyroid disease and low to no estrogen. I experienced a lack of proper sleep for almost two years and I had childhood trauma that I'd never dealt with.

Questions:

Do you realize the negative impact that lack of sleep can have on you? I didn't. How well do you sleep?

_____

_____

What are your thoughts and experience with the psychiatric unit? Positive, negative or indifferent?

_____

_____

_____

Have you ever tried to reach out for help? Did it make what you were going through better or worse? If worse, can you find the courage to reach out again?

_____

_____

_____

If you are struggling, who is one person you can reach out to? Can you try to find someone to help you build a team of people that will help you find life on the other side of suicide?

_____

_____

_____

If you have been struggling for sometime, is it possible to take a step back and think about what it is that you truly makes you feel alive? Often, this is tied to our purpose. Having purpose can be an anchor in the middle of the storms. What are your thoughts?

_____

_____

_____

Chapter Five

Acceptance: So You Can Live Again

Grief. Most of the time when we hear the word "grief," we think of death. Very few people realize that grief encompasses much more than death. On a broader scale, it's more about loss. Please think of the way this plays out in our everyday lives. When we lose a job, we experience grief. If we have a chronic illness or go through surgery, we experience loss. Breakups, divorce, kids growing up… these all can cause us to grieve. Most people, though, don't realize that there is a process in which we navigate grief. These stages are not linear.

Knowing the five stages of grief and allowing yourself to evaluate where you are in the stages can change everything. It can give you a focus on getting to the acceptance phase. You start living again when you have reached the acceptance phase. You know you've reached this stage when you no longer feel like an active participant or feel stuck; instead, you can look back on it as an observer. Acceptance allows us to feel joy without overwhelming guilt creeping in. Often acceptance requires us to hold both pain and pleasure simultaneously. Believe me, this does not come naturally, and finding someone to teach you how to hold both powerfully can be challenging. Holding both pain and joy is Ambivalence at its finest.

Looking back now, I see how in that two-year period of struggling with depression and suicide I was going through the five stages of grief even though no one in my life had died.

DENIAL• ANGER • BARGAINING• DEPRESSION• ACCEPTANCE

Denial showed up in the form of not really seeing how bad it was and how I let myself struggle silently for so long. I also didn't see how bad things were in my current environment.

I went in and out of **anger**. I was angry at myself that somehow I couldn't fix this. I was angry at God that such a creator would put any part of life in motion that would allow this, as well as the evil we've all seen. I was angry at those who continued to judge and point fingers. I was angry at the friends who left and betrayed me. I was angry at family members who offered no support. I was agitated at things I knew I shouldn't be annoyed at.

I began **bargaining** with God. God, is this a test? Is this some kind of punishment for what I've done? If I do this, will you save me from this hell? This fury? This maze?

Depression also showed up. It was Freud who first introduced us to the idea that depression was anger turned inward. Anger turned inward looks a lot like not loving yourself. I realized I held onto anger for so many things that weren't mine to hold, and I took that anger out on me. This awareness helped me see I didn't love myself and that I was addicted to being perfect. I wasn't sure why or its depth, but I began to see it was deeply related to my past trauma. I "decided" I couldn't be perfect or pretend I was anymore. I decided to look inward instead of outward to find my value. I started to believe I was deserving of love and respect despite the difficulties I was facing.

As I shared, up until this point, I unknowingly based my value on my outward appearance and obeying all the rules I felt one needed to live by to be a "good" person. Even though I was raised a Christian and knew that Jesus offered me forgiveness and freedom from self-condemnation, I still felt shame, guilt, and fear all of the time. I also placed my value in being a good mom, so when I "felt" like I was no longer a good mom, it seemed my life was over.

If we find our value in things that change, this can be a dangerous trap. I believe that this experience, my battle with suicide and going into the psychiatric unit, shattered the walls of perfection I hid behind and allowed me for the first time to see that people loved me even when I wasn't perfect or deserving of it. Oddly enough, I loved others who weren't perfect and had made mistakes. Why could I not offer myself that same love? All I can tell you is that from the moment I realized that loving myself was essential to surviving, I began to fight for me. I didn't know it then, but I had just started to reach the **acceptance** phase. Compassion and acceptance became the foundation on which I committed myself to excellence, not perfection. It has been this foundation that I've had to come back to, time and time again.

> From the moment I realized that loving myself was essential to surviving, I began to fight for me.

During my time in the unit, I watched as people walked by me with schizophrenia and multiple personality disorder. If you were born with something you can't control or change, please hang with me as I share ways to accept and handle this. I know this is tough.

I remember reading a book about eating disorders and the author challenging the readers to look in the mirror naked and say out loud, "I love you." I had never done that before, and it was hard to do. To this day, there are moments when I'm speaking that I encourage others to look at themselves in the mirror and say, "I love you." The psychiatric unit will always be the place I began to extend love and forgiveness towards myself. When I am really struggling, I will look at myself "butt naked" and say, "I love you, Jennifer."

I remember having conversations with women who were letting men physically beat them, and they didn't know why they kept going back.

I remember a lady being brought in, and her pants were all torn up, and she asked if she could borrow a pair of my jeans. She put on my jeans and walked out of my room, and I never saw her again.

It may seem like I am just rambling, but I realized that for some reason my world was not as bad as it could be. I think part of it was that I started to feel like I could rebuild and find me.

But did "me" ever exist?

Reflections:

I know when I was young and in my twenties I had no concept of grief, acceptance or trauma. It was only after my personal struggles that I started to learn about these things. I also know that I never had a conversation with anyone about loving myself. Isn't it crazy that we have to study and pass a test to get a license to drive a vehicle, yet something as important as loving and taking care of ourselves is not taught in our schools and sadly, sometimes not in our homes?

Sometimes we try to hurry through the stages of grief, instead of allowing ourselves to feel what we need to feel. Often, we can go in and out of the different stages. Knowing this, don't get discouraged as you make your way through this journey. It will get better. I know it's hard to believe that right now.

Questions:

Before reading this book, did you know the five stages of grief? If so, did you realize that you experience grief with many life circumstances and not just with death?

_____

_____

_____

Do you have anything that you feel you might be grieving?

_____

_____

_____

Looking objectively at yourself, do you think that you may be stuck in any of the stages of grief? Do you have a top emotion that you struggle with? Anger, sadness, denial?

_____

_____

_____

Do you find your value (worth) in things that change: job, parenthood, marriage, or outward appearance?

_____

_____

_____

Have you ever looked at yourself in the mirror, naked, and told yourself, "I love you?" Try it. It feels odd and can be extremely hard to do, but it can also be very empowering.

Chapter Six

When Good Isn't Good Enough

In order to survive my years of suicidal thoughts, I had to battle with one of my deepest core beliefs. I had to decide my daughters were better off with a broken mother, one who wasn't perfect and had to learn not to hide her imperfections. I learned to be honest. I had to look in the mirror and figure out how to love myself, accept this new me, and work on myself each day. I had to decide that that reality was better than a mother who chose to kill herself because she was flawed, and she knew it. Understanding this has set the course of my life.

I figured out the balance. Excellence, not perfection, forged my new belief system. I created this mantra that hangs on my desk. If you want to defeat anxiety, depression, or mental warfare, you have to accept that mental health battles are won when you start where you are and REBUILD From The Inside Out.

Every one of us is in our own arena, facing our own life, adversity, and reality. Making the decision to love and fight for yourself will take courage. It will require that you start talking to yourself with kind, positive words. It will require you to challenge yourself more than ever. Showing yourself self-compassion is NOT weak. It's courageous.

I wrestled with this thought: What does it take to be good enough? Perfection, achievement, high status, good deeds? I learned to love myself when I **accepted** these truths: I would never be perfect, yet I was born with great worth (value), AND personal growth in the midst of adversity is possible.

Do you struggle with the need to be perfect? If so, can you see the difference between perfection and excellence?

Do you have a roar that you need to develop when you feel like you aren't good enough?

Do you have a strong inner voice that encourages you?

If not, don't stop challenging yourself and asking why not? You are so worth it!

ex·cel·lence | \ ˈek-s(ə-)lən(t)s \
~ the quality of being excellent
~ an excellent or valuable quality: VIRTUE.

Excellence is a talent or quality which is unusually
good and so surpasses ordinary standards.

For so many years, I wrestled with finding balance in my life. I wanted to love me but still find a way to work on myself. I fought against my black-and-white thinking. I created this "mantra" that helps me find that balance and reminds me of my core values. It hangs on my desk, and I have it here to share with you.

Lose the battle, WIN the War!

Balance of Justice and Compassion

I will hold to a set of standards, virtues or codes
that looks to do no harm toward others or myself.
I will be compassionate and try to understand WHO I AM.

(Take a deep breath.)
I will work toward being better today than I was yesterday.

Humility: Seeking to Understand Who I Am

I acknowledge that I am not all-knowing and
can't possibly know what others have gone through,
just like others can't possibly know all the events of my life.
Therefore, I will choose to be kind FIRST
in all circumstances and seek to understand.

I will look to honor and see myself in all of humanity.
When I look at myself in the mirror,
I will seek to understand that I am a physical,
emotional, spiritual, and intellectual being.
I was born with inherent value.
I was born with the capacity to choose LOVE or HATE!

(Take a deep breath.)
I will work toward being better today than I was yesterday.

I AM Unique

l celebrate things that make
me different and unique from others,
recognizing that sometimes a culture or
other people may not live like me or agree with me.

(Take a deep breath.)
I will work toward being better today than I was yesterday.

Evaluate Every Day

If I look in the mirror and recognize any behavior
that appears to do harm or does harm to others or myself,
I will act with fierce devotion for the rest of my life
to work toward being better today than I was yesterday.
Discovering that change takes time,
I will take responsibility for my own actions,
acknowledge the past that led me to this point
and look toward the future with HOPE.

(Take a deep breath.)
I will work toward being better today than I was yesterday.

Becoming the person you want to be
doesn't happen overnight.

It happens by getting up every day
and making the CHOICE to be that person…
AND…doing that every day for the rest of your life.

Reflections:

I know how hard it is not to listen to those who point their fingers at your imperfections. This truly has been one of the toughest skills to master. **In order to survive any kind of battle or personal struggle in life, you have to intercept the naysayers and your own negative thoughts and refuse to let them live in your mind.** No one else on this planet can do that for you. Be fierce about it.

Questions:

What are the thoughts that haunt you? What thoughts do you want to intercept and refuse to let live inside of your mind?

_____

_____

_____

Think of someone you love. Now think about something that person does that makes them imperfect. Do you love them any less? Now, try to see yourself the same way.

_____

_____

_____

Chapter Seven

Prepared

Life after the psychiatric unit didn't turn around overnight. In fact, I had to return to the unit several months after the first time. One thing I remember about that time was I discovered how vital a safety plan was. All that said, I can tell you that things continued to get better, month by month. Sometimes I felt like it was two steps forward and one step back, but overall it was better. I didn't feel the energy and enthusiasm that I once had prior to my battle with suicidal ideation, but the darkness, fury, and heavyweight had lifted. **I've never had a season in my life that was as dark as it was when I battled suicidal ideation for a year. As you read this chapter you may seriously question that statement.**

The two-year span between life in the psychiatric unit and the day that has forever changed my life reads just like the storyline in your classic heart-wrenching tragic film. As a couple, we took steps to try and start over and rebuild our lives. If you have ever faced a dark season in your own life, you might be able to relate to how messy and outright ugly it can get. Sometimes when I take in those two years and think about the weight of responsibility that Brian and I carried as 27-year-olds, I'm surprised either of us lived to tell you this story. What happens next is a real-life nightmare that no parent ever wants to go through.

On August 11th, 2004, my husband and one of my twin daughters were killed by a drunk driver. It was a warm August day, and we had just registered our daughters for school. Born and raised in Colorado, we moved out to Iowa for a little over a year, had just moved back to Colorado and our Uhaul was still packed. We were headed out to get school supplies. Knowing that Brian's mom was going to be there, I decided at the last minute not to go. I said, "you guys go without me." We were in the long, beautiful driveway of my mom and David's house. As Brian got ready to leave, Brittany, McKayla's twin, said to me, "one more hug, mom, one more kiss." And so I gave her one more hug and one more kiss. That hug, that kiss, those words—are the last memories that I have of her. Amber, who was sitting in the middle in the back seat, asked if she could sit in the front. I put her booster seat in the front, helped her in, and buckled her up. I kissed Brian on the forehead, and they drove off. I whispered a prayer, "Father, keep them safe." Ten minutes later, a drunk driver T-boned the driver's side to my car and instantly killed Brian and Brittany. Flight for life came and took McKayla to Children's hospital, giving her a 20% chance to live and Amber, giving her an 80% chance to live.

When the officers knocked on the door to my mother's house and asked if they could come in, I knew that my fear of why I had not heard from Brian was confirmed. I can remember exactly where I was when those officers told me that my "youngest daughter and husband" were killed in a car crash. As they said, "Your other two daughters are fighting for their lives down at Children's Hospital," I fell to my knees on the cold tile floor screaming hysterically in my mom's kitchen. Still to this day, I have no sense of time for all of this. Immediately, my mind went to my daughters, who were alone in the hospital. The officers stayed with us until they were sure that we would get to Denver safely.

On the truck ride down, my mom and I sat together in the back; David was driving. If you've ever watched a movie and felt that intense emotion that happens as you watch someone's worst nightmare come true; That is what it felt like on the way down to the hospital. I was trembling, crying uncontrollably, and my thoughts raced back in forth from what just happened and not knowing what was about to unfold.

In loving memory of Brian and Brittany; you are missed terribly.

The last picture I have of me and my three daughters.

When I arrived at the hospital, I walked into the first room to discover that Amber was lying in the bed, alive. Instantly my mind was confused. For hours I had thought my youngest (Amber) and husband were dead. I ran into the other hospital room to find McKayla. I recognized her immediately. It was Brittany, the smallest, not my youngest, who died.

As I stood there with my mom, looking at McKayla, my mind flashed back to my brother, hooked up to the machines, and in those few short moments, I knew the battle I was about to face. I have no words to describe this moment. Nothing. How do you possibly take in this absolute, chaotic and utter devastation? I will always cherish the memory I have of my mom and me sleeping in the bed in a small room the hospital provided for families who have children in the ICU.

The grief and despair I felt when they died was more than horrific. A part of me died that day. Yet, that pain and darkness were different than the time of darkness with suicide. With suicide, I felt as though my mind had been kidnapped, and I had no control of what was happening. Still to this day I have to carry the weight of loss and simultaneously choose to live.

With their deaths, I knew there was nothing that I could do to undo what had happened. I focused on what I could change instead of what I couldn't. Somehow, I was able to get through the denial and bargaining stage of grief reasonably fast. Their death left me with a lot of anger, pain, and sadness, and rightly so. For years following, I would sit alone in my car at the lake while my daughters were at school, and I would wail until I could barely move.

I wrestled deeply with the fact that I chose not to go with my family that day. My logical mind says there is a real chance we would have already been through that intersection if I had gone. Oh, the what if's right? These types of life-altering events can keep us stuck in grief if we don't know the way out. Back to chapter two—I could not change the past, so I learned to accept it. I didn't realize it then but looking at it now, I can see that I was fighting for myself. I knew in the deepest part of who I was that if I wanted to win this battle, I would have to apply all the lessons I had already learned. Again, my foundation of growth was built on self-compassion and acceptance. Asking for help and talking openly were essential during this time.

I thought a lot about doing drugs. I wanted desperately to escape the emotional pain I was feeling, it was life-altering. I was so stressed out. Instead of doing drugs, though, I went to my doctor. I made it a priority not to misuse the medication he prescribed. This allowed my body to come down from the heightened state of stress and trauma. I focused hard on not taking the anger I felt out on me, my loved ones or others. Therapy was a must and not just for me, but for my surviving daughters as well. Please, don't think for one minute that I am judging anyone who turns to drugs or alcohol as a way to escape the pain they feel. Emotional pain is a tough battle to fight.

Six years after Brian and Brittany died I had the courage to share my story with a group of law enforcement officers. I felt so sick to my stomach that day. It took years of practice to learn how to stand in that pain. That speech was the beginning of me stepping into my deepest purpose. Now, I regularly write and speak on grief, PTSD, mental health, suicide prevention, adversity resolution, and resiliency. When speaking, most people assume that my battle with suicide came after my husband and daughter's death. Yet, the reality is, my battle with suicide was three years before they died. That truth is what inspired me to write my first book… *Inside The Mind" of Suicide* back in 2017.

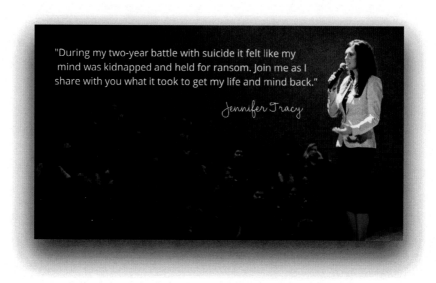

"During my two-year battle with suicide it felt like my mind was kidnapped and held for ransom. Join me as I share with you what it took to get my life and mind back."

Jennifer Tracy

I believe that my earlier battle with suicidal ideation saved my life and prepared me to know "how" to fight for myself and my surviving daughters when my husband and daughter died. Few people truly find joy, happiness, peace, and purpose on the other side of devastation. It was important to me that I not just survive this physically. Again, I believe that every poor choice, life circumstance, victory, and previous battle prepared me for this moment.

Working through my personal struggles with PTSD, grief and anger is what inspired me to create my community programs: Dare You To Move, Call For Back-Up and The Forgiveness GamePlan. These programs and speaking engagements gave me the platform to honor the pain I felt, and through those avenues I was able to see how I could use my pain and anger as a way to create positive change and teach others how to do the same.

Every strong tree has faced its season of darkness.
Jennifer Tracy

Often, I share that the day this tragedy happened, I was handed a pile of shit. I wasn't handed lemons and asked to squeeze them a bit and find some refreshing drink. No, I was handed a messy, stinky, pile of shit. You know what I've realized about it though? I've discovered after all of these years that shit can grow some really amazing flowers. We all have the **choice** to plant seeds in the mess. Every one of us. You, too, can find a way to honor your pain and life circumstances to create amazing things in your life.

It was an honor to be recognized by CDOT and
The Colorado Rockies for our speaking efforts across the state.

Reflections:

There are many ways to think about the negative or painful things that we go through in life. You've heard it said, "Is the glass half full or half empty?" Or, "The grass isn't always greener on the other side." Or, "Attitude is everything."

I'd like to challenge you to think about everything that you have been through, things that life handed you and even the poor or good choices that led you to this moment in time, RIGHT NOW! What if everything that you've been through has prepared you for your next step in life? What if not a single thing you've been through will be wasted? In order for this to be useful in your life it will require that **you make the choice to see it this way.**

Questions:

What is something that you have been through that looking back now you learned things that would not have been possible had you not gone through it?

_____

_____

_____

Though this may be tough to think about right now, how can you use the "shit" to grow flowers in your own life?

_____

_____

_____

Chapter Eight

Scars People Can't See

One year after my husband and daughter were killed, I was diagnosed with PTSD. When I was first diagnosed, I felt relieved. By this point, everything felt so complex. I tried to understand what I was facing and experiencing. With the label came answers, but also social stigma and confusion. I remember purchasing a very large self-help book on overcoming PTSD. Over the following years, I would use the book as needed and attempted to work my way through it.

Honestly, the massive amounts of pages paralyzed me. I also worked with my therapist and did EMDR (Eye Movement Desensitization and Reprocessing). During the time when my PTSD was the worst, I struggled with nightmares, flashbacks, depression, anxiety, avoidance, triggers, hyper-vigilance and irritability. I very rarely thought of suicide.

This is a hard chapter to write, and I hope that it's not too much for you as the reader. It is my truth though. I've lived through it.

For the first time in my life, I put on significant weight. I was so consumed with surviving and taking care of my daughters that the weight crept up on me, all 48 pounds of it.

Me during this time period

Things did not get easier for me as the following years passed. I remarried in March of 2007. This was a very happy time for me as it felt like a new beginning. I planned our wedding down to the last detail, including a 10 minute segment dedicated to Brian and Brittany through a video/ music compilation. In our first year of marriage we went through the unimaginable. My mother-in-law died in May of that year from brain cancer. I was very active in Jan's life and cared for her in the end stages. I remember thinking how beautiful it was to pray with her knowing she was dying. It brought both of us peace. I also remember thinking a lot about the contrast of her death, in which we knew what was happening, and had time to prepare, versus the sudden tragic death of my husband and daughter three years prior.

THEN that same year, my mother, Trudy, passed away at the age of 54. Ever since my birth, her kidneys were damaged. For several years she was on dialysis and eventually found a match for a kidney transplant. Stan, David's brother-in-law, was our hero. (Stan-thank you for your gift of life, you are an incredible man) My mom was weeks out after surgery, and all of us thought she was through the worst of it. After a transplant, there is a risk of the body rejecting the kidney, and she was doing great. Sadly, she had complications with her incision and ultimately died from a heart attack.

I will always thank God that I had been out at her house the day she died. I can remember every detail of my mom's room, the quilt on her bed, the prayer book she had by her bedside, and her favorite nail file. I had no idea that would be the last time I would see her alive. My mom was my rock. It was at that same beautiful home that I last saw Brian and Brittany. Her death, following so closely after their deaths, shook every person in my family, and no-one was left untouched. She was the most active and constant person in my life and my daughters' lives. For years following, I would pick up the phone to call her about a recipe, forgetting that she was gone. Sometimes I would call her voicemail just to hear her voice. Before we had her phone turned off for good, I saved her voice message on my computer.

My mom passed away three days after Thanksgiving in November 2007, and in December of that same year, one of my uncles, Danny, took his own life. I can remember sitting in the church's front row listening to the song Danny's sons picked out to play at his service. I wept uncontrollably. Even still today, when I hear that song, "Wherever You Will Go," I think of Danny, my cousins, their families and I pray for them. Sadly, I understood the suicidal mind.

As you can imagine, this was so much to handle in the first year of marriage with my second husband. I already had practice coping with grief and loss, whereas his mom's death was the most significant loss in his life. We were very unprepared to survive all of this together. Once again, I knew if I wanted to survive, I would have to fight for myself and Call For Back-Up personally. After my mother and Danny passed away, I found an incredible therapist in Loveland; I'm forever indebted to her. For several years she helped me process my complex grief and assured me that I wasn't crazy. During this time, both of my daughters went through different types of therapy as well. Amber and I did art therapy together, and McKayla attended week-long healing retreats for three years in a row.

After losing my first husband in a car accident, in 2011, my second marriage ended in divorce. Today, I hold no anger towards him. When he married me, I was in a time of brokenness and healing. As I grew through my trauma, I had become very active with speaking. He voiced multiple times that he wanted me to be his wife and not someone who talked about the past all the time. I couldn't understand that. I wanted him to be proud of me. I spoke of him in every speech as our Hero. As I write this, I know he would not want the life I have today. As a National Speaker, I travel, I have clients that message me in times of crisis, and I have periods of time where I'm deeply devoted to my work. All of which require me to use my past experiences.

I had been in therapy for years, and it was during a session with my therapist that he said, "I don't think I want to be married or work on the marriage anymore." Something snapped in me that day. That was August 2010. I unknowingly built a wall and thought - "I will probably never marry again." Divorce is a beast. It feels like death, yet sometimes you still see the person or run into them randomly. If you have children with them, that can make it even harder. I call this a "living death." The day our divorce was final, we both walked out of the courtroom. It was just the two of us. He hugged me. I was trembling. He kissed my forehead and said, "I'm sorry." As I shared, I hold no anger towards him. Reaching acceptance during this time was difficult for me. This was so much loss to go through. Outwardly, it may have appeared that I moved on, but it took me a long time to accept that he was not going to fight for me and that our life together was truly over.

THEN——As if life had not thrown me enough challenges, in early 2012, I suddenly lost the use of my hands and feet and had slurred speech from a Chiari I Brain Malformation. I had choking spells where I couldn't swallow. After several visits to specialists, the doctor determined that the only solution was surgery.

So, in July of 2012, I had a Chiari I brain decompression surgery and survived it. I now have a titanium plate in my head and like to call myself a metalhead, lol! (Seriously, I love listening to heavy metal music at the gym!)

February 2012- Loveland Colorado

As I write all of this, I can't help but remember the emotions that consumed me. Before my surgery, I sat down with both of my daughters and had to have an excruciating and heartfelt conversation with them about the possibility of me dying. I had plenty of life insurance money, and I wanted to make sure that I knew what both of their wishes were if I were not to survive. At the time McKayla was almost 18 and Amber was 14. We came up with several options, talked with those they would rely on, and wrote it all up in a will. The finality of all of this was surreal.

On the day of surgery, I remember Chief Wolfinbarger from Colorado State Patrol and his wife, Gina, coming to see me. I can't even put into words what that meant to me. I'll never forget a day previous that year where he pulled me aside after speaking live for a media campaign.

He said, "Jennifer, I would like to give you my personal Chief Coin because you are one of us. Thank you for all you do!" I had no idea then what an honor that was. Still, it took all my strength to hold it together in front of him. When I got back to the car with my daughters, I wept. That was the first of many coins I would receive. All of my coins mean such to me. The three coins below have significant meaning to me.

During one of my first conversations with Dr. Shauna Springer – or 'Doc Springer' as she is known to many, it was clear that she has been accepted in a similar way. We're both civilians, but we're not treated like outsiders. Doc Springer also has many challenge coins that symbolize the trust she holds with our nation's warriors. She once told me that when a recent fire threatened her home, her family photo albums and her challenge coins were the first things she grabbed on her way out the door.

In fact, Doc Springer committed to writing her book **WARRIOR** when a retired member of 5th Special Forces Group gave her a challenge coin during their final session. When he gave her this gift, he also gave her a letter. In the letter, he told her that she has the heart and spirit of a true warrior, not one who kills in battle, but one who fights for people and brings warriors home from war. He made her promise to "pull no punches" in sharing her observations and insights. Those who have read WARRIOR can see that she delivered on her promise to speak boldly, no matter what. Because of this courage, countless lives have been saved by her uniquely powerful insights.

The work we do – both my work and Doc Springer's – is our way to honor the sacrifices of those who fight for all of us. Another reason that we are so deeply dedicated to it is because this work is not about either of us. This is about being a part of something much greater than ourselves. It is about living into our deepest meaning and purpose.

When I was a little girl, I dreamed of becoming a mother and teacher. I loved to dance and sing. Not once did I dream about fighting battles. Honestly, I read books about being swept away by my night in shining armor. On the day my husband and daughter died, I stepped into an arena, one I never imagined I would be a part of. One I said I'd never survive should I find myself in it. The weight of grief from burying a child comes with a heavy life sentence.

What emerged in this arena was a woman forged by adversity—scarred by pain, shame and grief. Courage was my heartbeat. That tenacious strong will I had, just like my father, was routed deep in faith, determined to win. Though we've traveled different paths, we have both persevered with missteps along the way, it suffices to say that we can each point to the Sinatra penned mantra, "I did it my way." Every victory and failure had lessons to teach me.

As Chief and his wife sat by my side the day of surgery, I think they too knew the magnitude of the battles life had called me to fight. I'm not sure they understood, though, how alone I felt in my arena. Unlike him, I'd never been to Basic Training, had a unit, belonged to a tribe, team, or sisterhood.

On the day of surgery, all of my family and friends surrounded me. Within hours after my surgery, I had a severe reaction to the pain medication and remembered looking up at my daughters, who were next to the hospital bed. Amber was on my right side, and McKayla was on my left. Sharing this is so hard to do. I felt the life going out of my body. I saw a bright light. It all happened so fast. The only thing I remember is that I just kept saying out loud,

"No, no…no - I will not leave my daughters." Within minutes they gave me something to stop the reaction I was having. And as if that wasn't enough, with white compression airbags wrapped around my legs (used to keep me from getting blood clots) and 18 staples in the back of my head, I had to lay in an MRI machine for almost 45 minutes without any pain medication. Following that MRI, they immediately found a spinal fluid leak. They injected my blood into my spinal fluid, and I had to lay flat on my stomach for three days. All of this felt like physical torture.

I was in so much pain I wanted to die. All I could think of was McKayla and Amber. I didn't want to leave them. My love for Brittany and my mom beckoned me. I thought to myself, "Either way, I'll be ok." I have never experienced so much physical pain. Honestly, I'm not sure how I survived

I kept asking, "why God, why? Why must I continue to suffer?" I had always been a woman of faith, but it was then that my undying trust in my creator finally cracked. Somewhere inside, I felt ALONE. When I think of our Veterans and first responders, who have endured so much for us, it deepens my respect for them. I've worked with many who wrestle with their faith in God after the battles they have fought.
I left the hospital in a wheelchair. My youngest daughter Amber had to bathe me. I attended her high school open house using a walker. My oldest daughter McKayla had just started college. I relied on neighbors to take me to physical therapy because I couldn't drive.

My boyfriend at the time was a remarkable man who did all that he could to love and take care of me.

I want to be so clear about what I am about to say—**All of these life altering events didn't touch the depth of darkness I faced during that two year span (1999-2001) when I fought my battle with deep depression and suicidal ideation.**

> All of these life altering
> events didn't touch the
> depth of darkness I faced
> during that two-year span
> when I fought my battle
> with suicide.

Can you see that during all of these trials, as much as I suffered, my mind was intact? I was able to process all of this.

Sleep was a priority. I accepted what I could not change. I had strategies to fight mental warfare. Instead of avoidance, I would stand in the pain. I allowed myself to be angry yet looked for healthy ways to process it. Compassion towards myself was essential to my survival as I was the only one who knew my entire story.

I can't imagine battling all of this along with thoughts of suicide too. And yet I know for a fact that now after working with our First Responders and Veterans, this is often how they feel. They are expected to handle insane amounts of physical and emotional adversity. More often than not, if they ask for help, the unspoken message is, you are weak. They have so much to risk if asking for helps means they lose their jobs.

We have it all wrong. Men and women who work for years doing their jobs while battling thoughts that tell them to "just end it" are STRONG!

Each battle, though it took me down for awhile, made me emotionally stronger. With each blow, I looked for what I could learn. Pain can be an incredible teacher if you let it. I learned how to keep things in perspective and to fight like hell for myself. Battles can make your **courage** strong. There were days that I wanted to die, not because I was suicidal, but because I was so tired of fighting and I missed my daughter Brittany and my mom so much that I would give almost anything to see them again. I knew that would mean leaving my other two daughters—and that wasn't an option.

On the deepest level possible, I **accepted** the things that I knew I couldn't control. (Page 29) I learned a life-changing way to keep winning. I had to be OK with losing some battles as long as I stayed focused on winning the war.

"Lose the battle, win the war" became my mantra!…

Lose the battle, WIN the War!

When Brian and Brittany died, I made a promise to myself. This promise that I made is my War… I promised myself that I would do everything in my power to make sure that my surviving daughters would never have to say, "on the day my dad and sister died, my mom died too!"

I knew what that meant. That meant, no matter what happened, I would fight till the end for me, not hurt myself and not allow myself to become numb. That meant, despite my shortcomings, I would do my best to LIVE and lead them. I made sure they knew it was ok to be imperfect. When I failed I admitted it. I worked very hard to be balanced.

During those following years I struggled greatly with depression and anxiety. I felt an incredible amount of guilt and shame as I struggled in relationships. I was both warrior and wounded, and I knew it. I worked hard to live in the moment and enjoy being alive with my daughters. It meant everything to me to be at every school activity and sporting event with them. I never stopped sharing my story with attempts to help others. I kept looking toward the future with HOPE.

I wondered, how do I balance how I feel on the inside with the outside? How was I supposed to look and interact with people when I felt so messed up on the inside? On the good days, I looked normal as if nothing was happening. I struggled with how to show both sides of myself to people. Underneath all of this, I wanted so desperately, to be understood and feel whole again.

What if whole was never going to be an option? Could I accept this?

It was during this time that I created the "Forgiveness GamePlan." I needed a way to process my failure, regret, anger, and shame. Again, I had to go back to that foundation of compassion and excellence. Often I think people look at showing compassion as an excuse for poor behavior. I can only speak for myself regarding this, but showing myself compassion was in no way an excuse to continue poor behavior. Rather, this strategy is a process in which I learned to evaluate myself through the lens of compassion and recognize that change takes time. I have successfully used this technique to navigate the last eight years of my life.

Yes, I was one of those people with a handicap placard who looked like I didn't need one. What you can't see is the pain in my nerves from my brain surgery. It took me several years after surgery to regain the strength to drive and carry my groceries.

This is an interesting thing to ponder. In many ways, this relates to how our society deals with stereotyping or judging the people we meet and encounter everyday. For instance, when we see a homeless dirty person on the corner, we assume they are poor. When we see a well-dressed business person in an expensive car, we assume they are rich. Yet, you and I know that in many instances, the rich person may be on the brink of bankruptcy and the homeless person could be a war hero with a Purple Heart who can't find his or her way out of the darkness.

This, my friends, is what I call wisdom, knowing not to judge either the homeless person or the businessperson. Think about how each of my trials has offered me the chance to be kind to others, because I truly can relate to their pain. I carry this perspective with me each day.

Will you try this exercise with me? Imagine that you met me in the grocery store or gas station today. Imagine I'm wearing that pretty dress in this image. Instead of the distant look I have, imagine I'm laughing, smiling, and singing the words to my favorite song out loud.

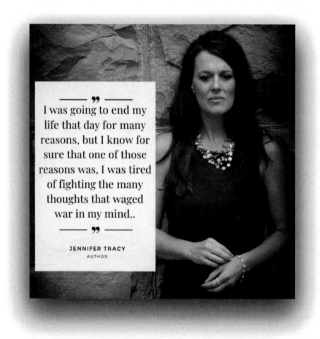

— 99 —
I was going to end my life that day for many reasons, but I know for sure that one of those reasons was, I was tired of fighting the many thoughts that waged war in my mind..
— 99 —

JENNIFER TRACY
AUTHOR

Inside "The Mind" of Suicide
Original cover photo from my book in 2017

Now stop and think about what you would conclude about me. Would you have any idea the things that I've been through just by looking at me? You can't see any of my scars, and when I'm dressed up and looking good, you wouldn't have a clue. This photo was taken by a dear friend, Paul, who captured me thinking about the suicide panel I had just been part of. Can you see how I might be judged by the way I seem to have it all together? What if the day we meet is one of the most challenging days of my life? An anniversary of a loved one passing? What if I need your kindness more than ever on that day? How would you know?

Brittany Anne-8 years old
I miss you so much!!!

On the flip side of this exercise, think about my daughter, Brittany, who died in the car crash. As I shared, she had Cerebral Palsy. Cerebral Palsy affects the brain and the way it sends messages to the muscles. Brittany's scars were pretty obvious to others. She walked, held her hands, and talked differently, and others made fun of her. I can recall many times people asking me, "What's wrong with your daughter?" Almost always, my reply was, "There is nothing wrong with her." Her brain and muscles work differently than yours and mine, and I would educate them further if they wanted to know. Brittany was judged by her different outward appearance. I think Brittany's wish would be that we were people who were kind. I can only imagine what life would be like if she was here with us today. I miss her so much. There are no words to express this pain.

Depression, Anxiety, PTSD and thoughts of suicide are complex. We can't see the battles that go on in each of our minds. We struggle to work through the scars that people can't see. People often struggle to communicate effectively about unseen battles. As a society we tend to make fun of our differences AND we have the audacity to penalize people when they seek help. Truthfully, those who battle depression, anxiety, and thoughts of suicide are some of the strongest people I know.

For me, change came in different ways at different times. During my first years of therapy, I was introduced to EMDR... EMDR changed my life. This type of treatment can be beneficial for processing trauma. It allowed me to tap into things that I had unknowingly buried in my mind, things that were triggering emotions, nightmares, and behaviors. Eventually I began to see how I could stand in the pain and not avoid it. This type of treatment was essential in overcoming my nightmares.

Change on a physical level came later. In 2012 after my brain surgery, my surgeon suggested that I completely change my way of eating. So, I cut out all gluten and decided to eat only whole foods, avoiding anything processed. Since then, I've lost 48 pounds, no longer have fibromyalgia and have better mental clarity. I still have to take medication to sleep at night and for my thyroid. Because of my Chiari I Brain Malformation, my pituitary gland is permanently squished.

Taking medicine is essential for my overall wellness. I started this book talking about "Victories on The Hill" because, as you can see, I have had to figure out my own personal solution, sometimes through the process of elimination, which includes **FAILURE.** True Resilience includes failure; why do we not like to talk about this? We all know that to become excellent at something we have to practice and fail. To become the best versions of ourselves it's essential to do this without shame, guilt, or societal pressure.

I'm not going to try and imagine what it was like for you to read this chapter. Honestly, I could write an entire book around trauma, pain, and grief. There is so much more to my story. As I shared at the beginning of this chapter, I know this was a lot. At times I still can't believe that I've lived it.

I know the deepest darkness… If I can survive it, so can you! Now go and fight for you. I believe in you!

8 years after surviving brain surgery- 2020

My deepest desire with this book was to take some my most painful life experiences and share with you what those things taught me. For many years I felt alone. Having spent the last 4-5 years working with individuals, couples and families; I no longer feel alone. Now, I'm the one who assures people, "you're not alone" and "you are not crazy."

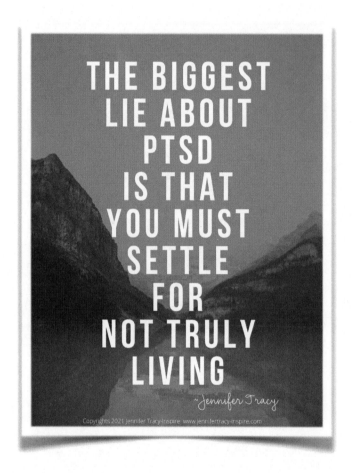

It would be my honor to share with you the rest of my journey. Battles lost and won to find VICTORY and HOPE.

Reflections:

Every one of us has scars that people can't see. We are human. It's impossible to not get hurt in this life. One way to master resiliency is to make your mind think about how to process daily defeat, personal struggles and the unfair things life hands us. In the end you have to decide how you are going to handle that. Lose the battle, win the war is a type of compartmentalizing. You decide in your mind that you can't win them all, but you stay focused on what's most important to you, i.e., "the war." We must not overlook that dark side of resilience that can breed the need to perfect. Instead, strive for excellence!

Questions:

What is a scar that you wish others could see and understand?

_____

_____

_____

What are the battles you've lost that you need to learn to let go of and forgive ?

_____

_____

_____

What is your "war"? What is so important to you that you would fight to attain or keep it?

_____

_____

_____

Chapter Nine

The Broken Golden Rule

Daily, I see people struggle with their own beliefs and choices. As I write this, I am aware that people are dying of natural causes and disease and some are dying as the result of another person's choices. Some of those choices are accidents, and some are the result of poor behavior and carelessness.

Life has thrown me so many things that I have had no control over, but as I shared, some of my struggles are also from poor choices that I made. As you know, my husband and one of my daughters were killed by another man's choice to drink alcohol to the point of severe intoxication. At this moment in my life, everything I believed was challenged, and, for a time, I walked a road I had never walked before. I threw away everything I believed in.

It was in those darkest moments of my life that I reflected on everything I had been taught, including my studies at Metropolitan State College, my faith and what I had learned from years of therapy, EMDR and self-help books.

What I concluded down this road was that, given my DNA and my environment, I very well could have been someone who struggled with alcohol addiction or living my life numb. At that moment, I saw myself in those who also struggled with their imperfections. I looked honestly at myself and asked myself, "What was it that I had successfully done not to be that kind of person?" On a profound level, I knew I was born with the capacity to choose; despite my "nature or nurture," I had to decide what I would do about it. This was not easy. I have had to make the choice to keep fighting for myself on so many occasions. I had to choose to not get stuck and angry—and fight for ways to be a person who, no matter what, could choose kindness, forgiveness, and love. Why? Because I knew I was desperately in need of those expressions from others, just like everyone else.

With God's help, I chose to forgive the man who killed my loved ones... but it was only because I had practice at forgiving those who didn't deserve forgiveness, and that included me. I haven't found anything more powerful than understanding "how" to forgive.

> It was only because I had practice at forgiving those who didn't deserve forgiveness, and that included me.

I believe the greatest gift we have is the power to choose.

Do you realize that your choice precedes every action you make? Love is simply a word on paper unless it's put into action.

I have a desire to see that people set aside their differences and instead focus on what they can control: The power in YOUR CHOICE.

It has been said that The Golden Rule is the one command that transcends many religions. The command says we need to love our neighbors as we love ourselves. Sadly, what we have is a society that doesn't love themselves—and therefore that's exactly how they are "loving" their neighbor. I call this The Broken Golden Rule.

I can almost see the irony of a person standing on the street corner yelling, "Love your neighbor as you love yourself," while secretly they can't stand to look at themselves in the mirror.

One of the most powerful moments in your life could be when you decide to stop yelling from the street corner, and instead, make the choice to learn how to love yourself, and then with fierce devotion—put love into action, by loving others. Revisit the mantra on page 57-58 and set goals around this. Remember, change takes time and dedication.

Reflections:

Imagine that you grew up in a home where "Love your neighbor as yourself" was the highest rule you were taught to follow. Now imagine that not only were you taught to follow it, but those that raised you lived it by showing you how it was done. They spent time with you, fed you when you were hungry, held you close when you were scared, taught you how to be brave, showed you how to enjoy the simple things, told you that you were amazing and believed in you and made giving to others a part of their life. This kind of love in a home is hard to come by these days. Is it any wonder that we don't do those things for ourselves and those we love?

Questions:

How do you see yourself in this broken Golden Rule? Do you love yourself the way that you wish you did? If not, why?

_____

_____

_____

How do you treat others? Is it easier to love others or yourself?

_____

_____

_____

What does "loving the me in the mirror" look like on a daily basis, for you?

_____

_____

_____

Chapter Ten

When God Ran

I was raised with the belief that I had a creator, and over my 46 years of life, I have taken the time to study different religions and philosophies. I've made it a point to be friends with as many individuals that I can from all walks of life and religions, including those who don't believe in a god and those who do. I have learned so much from my friends who have different beliefs than me.

There are some things in life you possibly can't understand until you experience them. Depression and especially suicidal ideation, found a way to make my entire body feel like I was a dead person walking in the shell of a body. I was used to feeling close to friends, family and God. During that time, I felt nothing. My mind remembered what it felt like to sing worship songs, but physically, I felt abandoned. There were so many times I just wanted to throw in the towel. During those years, I made choices I regretted, including walking away from everything I had put my faith in.

> Depression and suicide found a way to make my entire body feel like I was a dead person walking in the shell of a body.

Surprisingly, it was down that road where I found the God that to this day has shown me unconditional love. It was down the road of regret that God ran to me. God met me right where I was. I learned that unconditional love really did mean unconditional. As complex humans, it can take us a while to realize we are more than flesh and bones. There is something spiritual about us. Something in us longs for things this world just can't satisfy. I say this because during the dark moments of my depression I remember finding strength in something beyond myself. I would cry out, "Please give me strength to go on one more day," and somehow, I would find it. I learned that GOD can handle my doubt and anger. I used to feel guilty when I was angry at God or in general. I don't anymore.

With that said, I'd be a liar if I didn't tell you that I've had years where I doubted everything I believed and struggled to find hope. Despite my doubt and anger, my faith in God has sustained me through many dark nights. I would also fail to give credit where it belongs if I didn't share with you that the Bible, though hard to comprehend and seeming to be contradictory, has been the largest source of wisdom, hope, love and inspiration for me. Having God's word written on my heart has been an anchor for my soul.

I can't tell you how many times, though, I would leave a church or meeting with a Christ-follower and have to look up and ask, "Why? Why do they treat me like this?' It was a still small voice that would say, "That's not me, I'm sorry. I'm not condemning you!"

> It was a still small voice that would say "That's not me, I'm sorry. I'm not condemning you!"

When my husband and daughter were killed, Brian's mom received the life insurance benefit instead of my daughters or myself. On that day, my surviving daughters and I were left without a home, car or money. To this day we have never seen a single penny of that money.

Not only did she receive the life insurance money but she also used the fact that I had been in the psychiatric unit as a way to say I was an "unfit" mother and undeserving of my daughters. Her hateful actions were unjust. Both myself and my daughters (including Brittany) lived through unnecessary pain because of her.

Can you imagine the shame I already endured feeling so messed up during my battle with suicidal ideation yet having the courage to do the very thing we tell people to do- get help? And then to have that same thing used against me?

I want You back.
God

The greatest irony is holding the handwritten letter from the man in prison who killed my husband and daughter, thanking me for forgiving him. Compare this to the stark contrast of reality; my mother-in-law has never apologized, offered to help, or restore what she took from McKayla and Amber. After he died, she donated Brian's car and then dared to say, "How can Jennifer take care of her daughter's? She doesn't have a car." I tried to get some of our belongings from her through county court with no luck. She let our stuff sit outside her house and rust. I genuinely wonder, is she riddled with regret, or does she still think I'm unfit? Does she truly think my daughters would have been completely better off without me? Those were her intentions.

If this was a one time incident with her, that would have been different, but I had a long standing history of watching her completely cut out Brian's dad, over and over again. Even on the day Brian and Brittany died. I called Bob, Brian's biological father to let him know that the girls were in ICU. When he came walking down the hallway, she said, "who told him they were here?" I said, "I did, they are his grandchildren."

It took me so much longer to forgive her than it did to forgive the man who killed my husband and daughter. Honestly, it took me nine years to forgive her. All of this pain taught me valuable lessons on **remorse, hatred, and intention.** It's much easier for me to forgive even the most broken people who have no intention to hurt me than those who have intentionally harmed my daughters or me.

As you can imagine, this is a complex and sore subject, so I rarely share it with others—In fact, this is the first time that I've dared to share it so boldly. As I shared early on in my book, my intent is not to be malicious. I've had to think long and hard about the reason that I would share this with you. I came up with one compelling reason.

I can not in clean conscious sit here and tell you that I'm proud of all the choices I've made. I have made terrible mistakes and poor choices.
I also know that the only thing I can do is make things right with those I've offended and work hard every day to be better today than I was yesterday. It takes a lot of courage to look in the mirror and be honest with yourself. What do you think? What is it that keeps someone from apologizing and making things right?

I learned powerful lessons from those who betrayed me, judged me, and left us on the side of the road. I know how painful that was. I also learned that they, too, have a story, and so as hard as it was, I needed to forgive them. It was hard. It still hurts.

It has taken me some time to understand why people who walked in on particular chapters of my life judged me? Possibly, people assumed that somehow I did something wrong to be in such a mess. I wanted to share this for two reasons. One, people may write you off, but I believe that God never gives up on us. Two, during this time when we had nothing, my family and friends rallied together and helped us with so many things. My dad and Carol showed up to fight with me. My mom and David stepped up, my grandparents, Aunt Cinda… So many did. To this day, both Micah and Jodie have been a constant source of friendship and support. Another friend, Shelly, let me use her car for months until I could afford a new one. All of this was humbling.

> People may write you off
> but I believe that God
> never gives up on us.

The hardest part of it all was asking for help. I've had to tap into the power of teamwork so many times. I had to learn not to assume that people knew how bad it was because many people didn't see the back story. I'm forever indebted to everyone that helped us during that time. There is no way I would have had the inner confidence to stay and fight this battle had I not already mastered previous ones. Sadly, so many don't make it out of these encounters with injustice.

When I was younger, I think I held onto faith and hope because I wanted to believe that everything I had been taught was true. The hope of eternal life sounds wonderful. In contrast, if there is no eternal life, then I have to live with the cold hard fact that I will never get to see my precious angel, Brittany, again.

My faith today is strong. I don't simply believe because of the desire for eternal life. I believe because I've seen proof of love's power in my life. Time and time again, it has been my family and friends, people I don't know, churches and community programs that have lovingly supported me and my daughters. The number of individuals who have helped me is too many to count. I will never be able to claim that I made it here on my own. Even going through the "Ticket To Work" Program in 2014 to get off disability, though difficult, it brought me here today. What I can claim through all of these trials is that I had a choice, and I tapped into that power. I will always be able to say "I never gave up."

During my questioning and journey to find answers, I found a life-changing verse in the Bible. In Ephesians 4:26, I discovered something that's been powerful in my life. It says, "In your ANGER don't sin." It doesn't say, **don't be angry.** The Hebrew definition of "sin" is "to miss the mark."

As you can imagine, I have had to work though years of anger and pain on so many levels. What this verse tells me is that it is OK to feel angry, but I have to choose what I am going to do with it. I have to practice to not let my anger cause me to miss hitting the mark. Anytime we don't hit love in the center of the target we miss.

This was a game changer for me. I now realized I had a God who was OK with my emotions, pain and anger. I had a God who wanted to show me how to handle it. My God was near me, on my side.

> I had a God that wanted
> to show me how to
> handle it.

Abuse, trauma, depression, stress, death and suicide all have a way of shaking us to the core. Something else struck me in my core—the words to the song, "When God Ran," by Benny Hester.

I heard this song for the first time when I was 12. Some songs have a way of being written on my heart and soul. This is one of them. I remember when I heard it, it made me think and feel that God was loving. As I grew older and I saw the harsh reality of this life and desperately tried to be good and do good onto others, I think I forgot about the truth of this song. If the God in this song was real and true, then what he stood for was that I didn't have to have everything together in order to be loved.

It wasn't until after I ran away in pain and anger that I came to understand this truth. LOVE is always on your side. **Love may not approve of your actions but desires greatly to help you make a better choice next time. LOVE** see's our value and worth despite our inadequacies.

The only way I can put this into perspective is to think about my daughters. As I raised them, I would tell them what I thought was best for them. I disciplined them when they strayed, but I would say, "YOU own your choices. No matter what. No matter what life hands you, you get to decide what you will do with what that. If you do things you regret, own them. Forgive yourself and then go do something different. Never give up!" Throughout the years, I've made it clear to them that I cannot remove the consequences of the choices they make, but my love for them will not change, even if they choose a path of self-destruction. Is that not what LOVE itself is saying? No matter what, I'm here.

As I write this, the tears stream down my face. It hit's me in my core, "I'm here… I'm still alive…."

You may not believe that God is always on your side, and you don't have to. That is your right. BUT if you ever need some HOPE, borrow mine. I can tell you that I have run away, been rebellious and done it my own way. My personal belief is that you can never run too far where God's love won't reach you. Truly understanding this can change everything.

If you think that what you've done is too much, it's not. History is filled with people who've done things they regret, me included.

Adultery, murder, theft and lying; Those poor choices don't define you! You are not your past mistakes. We must face the consequences of our choices, but we are not defined by them. You can forgive yourself and make a new choice. Please, don't let the past define who you will be for the rest of your life. God will forgive you. It's never too late to make the next best right step. This song and many more have brought me so much hope. I've included the lyrics written by Benny Hester in his song,

"When God Ran." Listening to this song is powerful.

When God Ran

Almighty God
The Great I Am
Immovable Rock,
Omnipotent powerful
Awesome Lord
Victorious Warrior
Commanding King of Kings
Mighty Conqueror
And the only time
The only time I ever saw Him run
Was when He ran to me
Took me in His arms, held my head to His chest
Said "My son's come home again"
Lifted my face, wiped the tears from my eyes
With forgiveness in His voice
He said "Son, do you know I still love you?"
It caught me by surprise when God ran
The day I left home
I knew I'd broken His heart
I wondered then
If things could ever be the same
Then one night
I remembered His love for me
And down that dusty road
Ahead I could see
It's the only time
The only time I ever saw Him run

When He ran to me
Took me in His arms, held my head to His chest
Said "My son's come home again"
Lifted my face, wiped the tears from my eyes
With forgiveness in His voice
He said "Son, do you know I still love you?"
It caught me by surprise
It brought me to my knees
When God ran
I saw Him run to me
And then I ran to Him
Holy One, Righteous Judge
He turned my way
Now I know He's been waiting
For this day
And then He ran to me
Took me in His arms, held my head to His chest
Said "My son's come home again"
Lifted my face, wiped the tears from my eyes
With forgiveness in His voice
I felt His love for me and then He
Ran to me
Took me in His arms, held my head to His chest
Said "My son's come home again"
Lifted my face, wiped the tears from my eyes
With forgiveness in His voice
He said Son, He said Son, My Son
Do you know I still love you
Oh He ran to me
When God ran

Lyrics shared with permission by Benny Hester

Reflections:

Stop for one minute and think about your fingerprint. In all of creation, there is only one that matches yours. YOUR fingerprint is so unique it can be scanned and traced to you whether you are in Africa or Atlanta. When you stop to consider all of the life circumstances that have brought you to this moment, is it any wonder that you would have a personal unique relationship and set of beliefs about gods or God?

Has it ever occurred to you that when you ask God for help he has to deal with you the same way you do? He has to help you with the physical, mental, emotional and spiritual parts of you! This is why I have included the worksheets at the end of this book. Take some time to look at your own life through this lens.

Questions:

What are your personal beliefs about God, a higher power and love?

_____

_____

_____

What have you experienced that makes you have belief? Has anything happened that causes you to not believe?

_____

_____

_____

For those of you that do believe in God: When did you first believe? Do you know why you believe the things you do? Do you think it's possible to run so far from God into the darkness, that God can't reach you?

_____

_____

_____

_____

God's Mercy Seat; High Above Manoa Valley, Oahu, HI

Ho'oponopono Mantra-

"I love you. I'm sorry. Please forgive me. Thank you."

Chapter Eleven

Lasting Change

Looking back now, it's clear something was not working during the years where my depression took a turn toward suicide.

Who goes to therapy, is on medication and still walks around feeling guilty, hopeless and alone? Sadly, I think many people are walking around feeling this way today. All of these life events inspired me to think about what I did to make it through not just this devastating time period, but so many more following it.

Underneath everything I believe, and now teach, are several foundational truths. Lasting change, or surviving "The Fury" or any storm in life, requires three things:

- You have to want to change.
- You have to believe the change you desire is possible.
- You have to have the resources to accomplish what you desire.

Have you ever met someone who wanted to change something in his or her life? Think about what kept them from finding lasting change. I believe most people who are suicidal desperately want to change. I believe most people, not all, end up taking their lives because they no longer believe that what they want is possible. They lose HOPE. If they've tried several things and none of them worked, they reach a point where they can no longer go on. I can't speak for other people, but I refused to quit looking for help. I get why people do though. I've been at that point so many times. I also believe that because of the depression and pain they are experiencing, some continue their self-defeating behaviors. Again, this just adds to their ongoing mental pain. Sadly, there are so many hurtful messages said in society. It breaks my heart to learn that good-hearted men and women walk around struggling silently.

Usually, when I share with people that I forgave the driver who killed my loved ones, they say there is no way they could forgive. I think people don't realize you can forgive someone and still feel angry. Webster's dictionary says to forgive means you stop holding that anger towards the offender. What good would it do me to be angry at him for the rest of my life? He can't ever give me back what I want. Can you see how I separate the "offender" from the poor choice or behavior? I still feel angry. Watching my daughters suffer is so painful. What would happen if you learned to channel the pain and anger into something positive? Converting this pain is what I have done. When I'm angry, I look for ways to use that positively. Can you also see how sometimes, you are the "offender" in need of others to stop holding their anger out towards you? I know I do.

Looking at it from the other side, I understand why some people in this situation become mean and angry. The storm and darkness that is fought inside the mind every day is a tough battle. If you have never felt this way or battled with this type of mental warfare, I can only hope you will think twice before judging someone who has. People who feel others are better off without them are not thinking clearly and tend to feel alone and so isolated.

So after all of this, how in the world do we find lasting change?

Think about something that causes you conflict or something you want to change about yourself. Now, keep that in mind as you answer these questions.

Ask yourself, do I really want to change this? Am I committed to change? Be honest if the answer is "I'm not ready to change."

Next, ask yourself, do I believe that change is possible in regard to what I want? Am I hopeful I can accomplish this?

Lastly, figure out what it would take to create lasting change in this area. Is it money, taking classes, joining a support group or changing your environment, perspective or education?

Lasting change usually requires having many tools and resources.

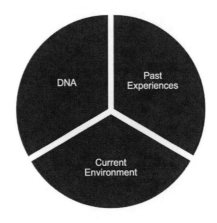

Self-Evaluation

When considering how to help yourself in regard to mental health issues, start by evaluating these things.

Can you pinpoint when you started to have thoughts of suicide? Or when anxiety or depression started for you?

Have you been evaluated physically? Is it something connected to your DNA or genetics? Is it something emotional from your past? This can be second-hand trauma as well. Is there something in your current environment that is causing this or adding to it?

DNA

_____

_____

PAST

_____

_____

CURRENT

_____

_____

Reflections:

I can confidently tell you that in most areas of my life I'm better than I was. I'm not where I want to be in some areas, but I'm aware of it. I'm compassionate towards myself with things I'm working on for two reasons. One, I give myself credit for what I've been through—my wins. Two, I'm not in denial about my struggles; I can honestly say that I work on them. Isn't that all we can ask of ourselves on this side of trauma and grief? To stay committed to growth.

Stop long enough to ask yourself, "What's going on with me? Why am I acting this way?" Your anger, pain and struggles are connected to **something**. It will help you overcome the battle in your own mind about "who you are" versus "what you do, think and feel."

If you keep making poor choices, own it. Ask for help. Keep trying. Forgive yourself and try again.

Questions:

What is something you want to work through? Addiction, self-harm, self-hatred, pride, anger?

_____

_____

_____

Say this out loud: I don't know how I will attain _____
(fill in what you are working on) I only know that I will.

This is a positive affirmation.
Writing this out and hanging it on your mirror can be useful as well.

Chapter Twelve

Check-Engine Lights

Back in 2016, I had a thought come to me as I was driving. I started thinking about how our minds and bodies are a lot like the motor vehicles we drive.

The check-oil light and check engine light are designed to help us know when something in the vehicle needs attention. Our bodies are very similar. In the psychiatric unit, they called these red flags. I like to think of depression, anxiety, thoughts of suicide, and pain as the lights on the dash of my car. It makes it seem so logical, and therefore, it is easier to reach out or start a conversation about finding solutions.

Almost all owners of any vehicle know that when any of the lights come on, you should pay attention to it immediately. Typically, unless you are a mechanic, you take your vehicle into a shop and do a diagnostic test. We have been taught that if you continue to drive your vehicle while the check-engine or check-oil light is on, you have a high risk of your car breaking down.

What would happen if people started to pay attention to the thoughts inside their minds and simply checked in to see what was going on? Acknowledge the lights: no stigma, no pressure, no judgment. Honestly, I designed every chapter in this book to be like a diagnostic test. My hope is that you would have an aha moment somewhere throughout these pages that would bring clarity to what you or someone you love are facing.

Would things change in our society if we stopped judging the "check engine" lights and instead focused on creating a safe and effective place where we could evaluate why those lights were on in the first place? When I think about what I have done over and over, it truly has been— Run a diagnostic test. Learn to Recalibrate. Rebuild myself from the Inside Out. Recalibrate. Rebuild.

If I'm honest, I've been the woman who was incredibly resilient and then found myself NOT so resilient. During this time, it was difficult to convince me that I was not a burden when my car was breaking down on the side of the road, spark plugs were hanging off, and smoke was coming out of my engine every week.

re·cal·i·brate/ˌrēˈkalibrāt/
verb calibrate (something) again or differently

To make small changes to an instrument
so that it measures accurately.

Ongoing trauma and stress can sometimes lead us to make choices we regret. When we are sitting in a mess, possibly one we might be responsible for, **it's essential to separate our worth from our behaviors.**

If this is you- you have to learn how to enlist help with the indicator lights and engine. If you already knew how to fix things on your own, you would have done that by now. Stop being stubborn. YOU ARE NOT BROKEN. The sooner you reach out and run a diagnostic test, the greater the chance you'll have at finding a solution. You can REBUILD.

If someone you love is struggling with an engine that is not working- I believe what they need to hear the most is that they still have value and worth, especially if they make the brave choice to go and get their "car" fixed. Reassure them you will stay by their side and that it's possible to REBUILD. The dark side of resilience can sometimes cause us to override these lights and continue to drive. As I've said, resilience without proper care can be deadly, I know. Please don't struggle silently.

Reflections:

As hard as it is for me to face, I've had to ask myself, "What would have happened if I had not asked for help the day that I was ready to kill myself?" What would have happened if in my crisis I did hurt myself or those I loved? I'd then feel more guilt and more shame. This is why it's so important to take care of the "lights" right away and never stop fighting until you figure it out.

Will you help me spread the message about depression, anxiety and suicidal thoughts being like the lights on the dashboard of our vehicles? The sooner we address and assess what is going on, the greater chance we have at preventing a complete breakdown on the side of the road or a total loss.

Questions:

Have you ever been in the vehicle when the check-oil or check-engine light has come on? Were you or the person driving more concerned about fixing the vehicle or about the light itself?

_____

_____

_____

Can you think of a place where you can check in and talk about mental wellness without the fear of judgment?

_____

_____

_____

Chapter Thirteen

Would You Take Insulin…
If Your Life Depended on It?

While I do feel there are multiple ways to treat a specific illness, there are times you should use the most efficient form of help to save your life.

My approach to medication stems back to my belief of looking at a person as a whole. I think it is important to remember we are all born with a different set of DNA, and who we are, to a large degree, is shaped by the environment we grew up in.

I personally struggled with the fact I was taking an anti-depressant medication until I thought about how there are many instances in my life where I wouldn't think twice about taking a prescription drug, such as insulin for diabetes.

I would like to consider being diagnosed with diabetes as an example of how you can use medication and then make some lifestyle changes in order to correct your health issue. The opposite of that also is true. There are some cases in which once you are diagnosed with type 1 diabetes, you must take insulin and manage your sugar intake for the rest of your life in order to save your life.

In the case of diabetes, there are many factors that come into play with the treatment and diagnosis of it. For instance, some people genetically inherit diabetes, and no matter how well they eat, they will need to take insulin to stabilize their blood-sugar levels. Just like diabetes, there are many types of mental illness that require you to take a medication for the rest of your life to correct an imbalance in your body. A few examples are bipolar disorder and schizophrenia. In contrast, if you have lived most of your life without feelings of depression or thoughts of suicide and find yourself struggling with these, there are many ways to try to treat it. It's very important to establish a good relationship with your primary care physician when working through this. I don't say this lightly. I've had some very awful doctors who've made my life worse. I am truly grateful for my primary care doctor. His patience and wisdom have provided a safe place for me to find ways to keep moving in a healthy way.

I had to make myself think of taking my medication as if I were merely taking insulin and how, if that was the case, I would feel no shame in needing to do so. Now, it's easy for me now to overcome the stigma of needing to take medication. It wasn't always this way, and I know for a lot of people it's not that easy.

There have been periods of time, years even, since my husband and daughter's death where I did not need to take an antidepressant at all. I've tried so many times to try alternative ways to sleep without taking medication, and after months of struggling, I knew I had to return to taking the medication in order to sleep. I have successfully taken a small amount of an old antidepressant, Amitriptyline, to sleep now for close to 13 years.

Since that fierce battle with suicide, I have developed a safety plan for myself. I look at thoughts and behaviors now as red flags or "check-engine" lights that are saying, "Hey, you need to pay attention to this." I don't feel shame or guilt about this. Not now. Not anymore. I fight through whatever's in front of me to make sure I get myself back to the place where I'm out moving and living again.

Reflections:

For generations, we have treated mental health differently than other illnesses. There is scientific evidence to support how important getting proper sleep, proper serotonin and how eating healthy foods are to maintaining strong mental health. Despite this knowledge, people will go months, even years, without sleeping well, feeling depressed and struggling silently with thoughts of suicide. Like I said earlier, I am not saying that taking medication will prevent all suicides. What I am saying is that we must learn to fight for ourselves and make sure we do whatever it takes to be healthy. For me, that means taking medicine prescribed by my doctor.

Questions:

What are your thoughts about having to take a sleeping medication? If you have been struggling to sleep for months or years, would you consider talking to your primary care physician about it? If you feel hopeless or depressed, would you consider talking to your primary care physician?

_____

_____

_____

If you have been struggling with depression, anxiety or thoughts of suicide and fight this battle alone, would you consider finding the courage to open up about this?

_____

_____

_____

What do you think? Would you feel shame if you had to take insulin to save your life?

_____

_____

_____

Chapter Fourteen

Lessons from the Rich Man Who Had It All

During a group therapy session, I remember a man in his thirties saying he had all of his needs met. He had a successful career and a great family and home, but he couldn't understand why he was suicidal. He didn't want to be there with us in the psychiatric unit, and he had no idea why he couldn't fight and figure it out.

This story profoundly shaped the way I view mental health. Not everyone has a horrific childhood to trace back their pain and fury to. Not everyone who is struggling is poor or an addict. Sometimes it's a health issue. Sometimes it's just plain biological. And sometimes it's unhappiness, and you have no idea why.

While I can't remember the name of this man, obviously his story stuck with me. I think it hit me so hard then because I had so many obvious reasons to be suicidal—surgery, hormones, abuse and trauma. I wanted to share this story to make a very real point.

Sometimes, there is no obvious reason that you are having thoughts of suicide. That doesn't make your situation less valid, real or dangerous. Honestly, not having something to pin them to can be disturbing and scary. No matter what, remember you are not your thoughts. Honor the thoughts just like you would the lights on your dashboard and find the courage to go get help. It's not your fault. Don't let this stop you from seeking a solution.

Reflections:

Many times people think that the grass is greener on the other side. We may think that having money would solve all of our problems. I think we can look back in history and see that many famous, rich people have struggled with depression, anxiety and suicide as well. Don't allow yourself to get caught in the trap of thinking that happiness and the way through your current experiences is always on the other side of the fence.

Questions:

Where do you see yourself in this story?

_____

_____

_____

Have you ever judged someone by saying things like, "What is your problem, you have everything you need?" or "Suck it up, this is all in your head."

_____

_____

_____

Does there seem to be no reason for the depression or suicidal feelings that you have been dealing with? Are you struggling silently?

_____

_____

_____

Chapter Fifteen

Addictions and the Hold They Have on Us

I have been asked on many occasions by those who have lost loved ones to suicide, "Why did you not kill yourself and my loved ones did? What saved you and not others?"

As I've already shared, suicide, depression and suicidal ideation is complex. I only have my personal journey through it to share with you.

What I'm about to say isn't intended to offend you, especially if you struggle with substance abuse or are using alcohol or drugs to cope, or if someone you love has struggled or does struggle with substance abuse. During the greatest trials and struggles of my life, I never turned to drugs or alcohol. I believe this is a large reason that I am still alive today.

I don't share this to make you or others feel guilty for turning to drugs or alcohol. Quite the opposite. I share this because the amount of shame and guilt I felt already was so awful, I could see why people turn to something to stop the pain. And, I can see how turning to things to stop the pain creates a vicious cycle that adds even more to the regret, guilt and shame. I love now and have loved in the past many people who struggle with substance abuse. I believe people are born with a predisposition to addiction. Addiction is a beast. If this is your "war" remember the difference between excellence and trying to be perfect.

One reason I didn't turn to drugs or alcohol was that I thought about it critically. Having such a clear image of what happened to my brother has always stayed with me. Again, that pain was my teacher. I would say to myself, "Jennifer, if you get high, when you come down from that high, your pain, this reality, will still be here." At first, I felt so stuck because I wanted the pain to end, but I didn't know how to stop it. As my reader, though, I want you to know that I genuinely believe if I had added drugs or alcohol to the mix of what was already a fury, I'm not sure I would have been able to think the way I did about things and to continue to fight for myself. I'm not sure I would have had the mental clarity to walk myself into the ER and ask for help. This is important! Its scientifically proven that low amounts of serotonin in the brain cause depression.

Many people, when they are depressed, self-medicate by using drugs and alcohol. So many of our first responders, veterans and those who can't access help without the fear of losing their jobs use alcohol as a way to sleep. *Alcohol is a depressant*. While you are intoxicated or high, you are providing yourself with the time to not think about what is upsetting you. It allows a short-term escape from reality. The problem, though, is that when you are not drinking, you have put yourself into a more depressed state. Not to mention if you drink a lot, you probably are dehydrated as well. Alcohol is not the answer to helping your mind and body cope with the things you are going through. Fight with all that you must to find other ways to cope. If you struggle with substance abuse, don't lie to yourself about it. Face it. Fight through it. You are not alone and so worth the fight!

If you or someone you know struggles with substance abuse, I want you to know that even though I've never been addicted to any substance, I've had many surgeries which required I take pain pills. On more than one occasion, I had to fight hard to get off those and I know what the withdrawal symptoms are like. The withdrawal symptoms alone are hard to fight through. Addiction is a tough battle. If you or someone you love struggles, I'm sorry. It's not a sign of weakness. All I can say is it's never too late to be who you want to be.

This is one promise that I have been able to keep. It has not been easy to say the least. Even sharing this is hard. Making the choice to feel is no easy thing. When I consider everything that it took for me to survive, I can't think of anything more powerful than my mind. I had to change the way I thought about so many things. I had to admit that I didn't love myself. I had to admit that I had a wrong perception about God. I had to admit that I needed help in so many areas of my life. I had to admit that I needed to challenge the thoughts I allowed myself to think. I had to learn how to fight to protect my mind, body and soul.

Reflections:

Changing the way I thought and saw myself changed everything. If my mind was a battlefield, there was mental warfare going on constantly. As I began to challenge and rewire the way I thought, I can honestly say, I truly started to love me. It was then, in the darkest time of my life, that I changed the relationship that I had with myself. I learned to fight for me. One of the hardest things to do is to find compassion toward yourself in the struggle. I know, during times of poor choices we can be so hard on ourselves.

> If my mind was a battlefield, there was mental warfare going on constantly.

Questions:

What is one thing that you are proud of? Do you have something that you have worked hard to achieve?

_____

_____

_____

How would it feel to fight for yourself? Does this feel selfish?

_____

_____

_____

Do you have a family history of substance abuse?

_____

_____

_____

Do you struggle with substance abuse? Do you know how to tell if you do or don't?

_____

_____

_____

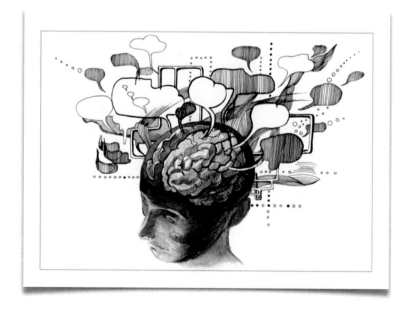

Chapter Sixteen

Tell the Truth, the Whole Truth and Nothing but the Truth

In July of 2016, I set out to write my personal story with suicide that I had fought through back in 2001. Little did I know that when I started to write this book that I would recall things I had forgotten. Honestly, I underestimated the emotional toll it would take on me to dig back that far to share with you those moments in my life.

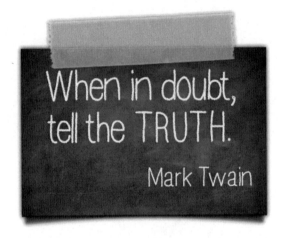

In 2017 when I published my first book, I wanted to share with you the whole truth and nothing but the truth. Writing my original book was traumatic for me and I didn't consider how that would affect me when I set out to write it. I enjoy writing and thought I'd have this book done and published in no time. Naively, I also thought since I talk about this all the time, why would writing about it be any different? Since I had proclaimed to the world that I was "writing this book," the pressure to finish this book overrode the "check-engine" lights as I like to call them.

So, the honest truth is: I found myself struggling with thoughts of suicide as I continued to write my first book in 2017. At first, it didn't bother me much. As I explained earlier, since the time that my husband and daughter died, I've had periods of time where I struggled greatly. This wasn't anything new or bothersome to me. Almost always though, if I give the thought a voice, dig deep and ask myself where it was coming from, the thought would go away. However, this time that didn't happen.

As the thoughts continued to persist, it messed with me, A LOT. Here's why! I was watching my public speaking career take off, running community programs focused on PTSD, mental health, grief, suicide and overcoming adversity. It hit me, I had a lot to lose if being suicidal meant I could lose my career. STIGMA was staring at me in the face! FEAR glared at me with intent to win!

You see I realized I wasn't afraid of the thoughts. I knew I wasn't my thoughts. I had already won that battle. I was afraid of anyone that "would judge me or seek to take away my career." That's why I kept ignoring the light.

> STIGMA was staring
> at me in the face!
> FEAR glared at me
> with intent to win!

Not for long, though. As the thoughts of suicide or "check-engine" light remained on, I remember thinking to myself, "Jennifer you dare people all the time to go get help when the light stays on, so what is it that you would tell them to do in your case?" It was during this moment in time that I understood how hard it was to ask for help when you know that your career, children, everything that you've worked so hard for, could be gone.

I thought about what it is that I would do or tell others to do in this particular case and then, I worked hard to do it. Not all at once, but I took these steps:

- Eat well
- See my therapist
- Practice kindness toward myself
- Take a step back and time off if needed
- Meditate and/or pray
- Talk to my primary care physician
- Focus on what I could change
- Know the 5 things I can't change
- Create a team of safe people I could talk to
- Develop an emergency plan
- Evaluate what part of this was from my past, what part of this was physical and finally was there anything in my current environment that was adding to this.
- Get involved in some type of community: Church/Support group

The hardest thing on that list for me to do was to walk away from the book for awhile. It took almost five months until I was ready to finish it. The second hardest was for me to get involved in a community where I could find support, I was so afraid of being judged again.

Then the next biggest obstacle I struggled with was: Should I share this part of the story in my book? Again, back then, I was deathly afraid that if being honest meant my career was at risk, I feared sharing the truth.

I spent months thinking about this. I thought about the risk. I thought about my reputation and what I could lose regarding my career. I also thought about what was more important to me, my pride or being honest about how hard it is to be real?

> I thought about what was more important to me, my pride or being honest about how hard it is to be real.

What do you think? Did the thoughts of suicide disqualify me from doing my work? Or would the behaviors, actions and choices I make that followed the thoughts disqualify me? Personally, I feel it would disqualify me to continue in my line of work only if I chose to do nothing about my thoughts.

And isn't this one of the biggest questions we face? Because you see, how you answer that question on suicidal thoughts changes everything.

So, on a broader level I'll ask another question.

Does having a mental illness or suicidal thoughts disqualify me or anyone from our everyday jobs and lives?

Or would the choices, actions and behaviors that follow these situations disqualify us? **Why would doing the right thing cost us?**

This, THIS... is what I have come to believe... whether it be anger management, depression, addiction or self-harm, what we need more than anything is to understand on a deep level that we are not our thoughts, and our personal struggles do not disqualify us to keep moving forward in life. We have value and worth despite our inadequacies. **What disqualifies us is choosing to do nothing**. Having moral courage means you do the right thing no matter what the cost is. This includes getting help for yourself.

Personally, I think what disqualifies us is believing the lie that we should hide and be ashamed. What disqualifies us are our ACTIONS, not our thoughts. What disqualifies us is not acting as soon as the "engine lights" come on, causing a break down. Yes, you and I both know that there is a double standard. Don't give up. Don't believe the lie that you are alone and that it will never get any better. It can. My life is proof that you can make it through the darkest times of life and find beauty, purpose, hope and strength in the pain.

In regards to work, your life is more important than your job. If you are afraid of losing your career, you can't work if you are dead. Nothing, I mean nothing, is more important than your life. Not even your career. It's one thing to lay down your life in regard to saving someone or if your line of work requires such a thing. However, thinking that depression, anxiety, addiction, hopelessness, thoughts of suicide are things we must accept is the farthest from the truth. The sooner you address these things the greater chance you have of sustaining both the career you love and the people you would die for.

> Your life is more
> important than your job.

In some cases, I understand the situation you face means you may have to step down from your job, but your life isn't over. Please don't believe the lie that tells you it is. I know how hard the decision is to get help. I've worked really hard to be where I'm at today. In 2005 I struggled with 80% of the symptoms of PTSD. Today, I successfully manage 20% of those symptoms. Primarily those being anxiety, triggers and flashbacks.

When I walked into that psychiatric unit 20 years ago, I was hopeless that change was possible. I had tried everything I could to stop the thoughts and the vicious cycle I was in. There was only one thing I had not done yet, and that was to completely surrender and admit that I couldn't fight any longer without the help of others. You see, I was missing two of the three key components I now believe must be there for lasting change to happen. I was hopeless and I had run out of further resources to change my situation. The resources were there. I just had to keep fighting until I found the ones that worked for me.

And, during my short battle with suicidal thoughts in 2017 I evaluated for myself those three questions for lasting change again (see page 103).

Did I want to change? YES!

Did I believe it was possible? YES!

It was the third piece that I needed. I knew I needed resources to help me. I also asked myself the three self-evaluation questions (see page 104). Were my suicidal thoughts stemming from something from my DNA or something physical, from my past (emotional) or from something in my current environment?

I had my primary doctor check me out physically; all was well there. I checked in with my therapist and we felt that this struggle was possibly from the stress going on in my current environment; i.e., personal stress and the stress from writing this book.

One month after walking away from my book the ongoing thoughts of suicide lifted. It was hard to do this. Because of my previous battle I knew what I needed to do and I was able to stay safe while I worked on everything that was on my list above. Through all of this I remained focused on my speaking and community programs; in fact, I had over 15 speaking engagements January through May.

Boldly I say, all of this was worth the effort it took to survive.... YOU are worth it! Don't give up.

So, what does all of this have to do with you and the current situation you find yourself in?

Well, everything! So many of us are fighting battles that people have no clue we are fighting. We all have something we are working to change.

Why are you reading this? What were you hoping to find here? Whatever the reason you picked up this book and whoever you are, I hope you know how truly unique and special you are.

I hope I have inspired you to think differently.

It's my hope when you think of me that I inspire you to cry and wipe your snotty nose on your pants and do it without shame. I can't tell you how much I cried writing this book.

I hope you find the courage to look at yourself in the mirror, despite what the number is on the scale, and say, "I love you. I love what's beautiful and what isn't. Believe you can change!"

I hope I inspire you to visit the places that have caused the most pain in your life and to stand there with strength and courage and look at that place and ask yourself how you can use that very pain, that very darkness, the thing that was meant to destroy you and realize you, too, can grow flowers from your own pile of shit!

I hope I inspire you to talk openly with others about the things that haunt you and the things that scare you the most.
I hope if you're struggling with addiction, a mental health issue, chronic pain, grief or anything that causes negative energy in your life and you realize that your "check-engine lights" have been on for too long, I hope I inspire you to get help. Choose "prison" (psychiatric unit) or a type of specialized treatment center if you must to save your life, because it's

better to be broken than to not be at all! Today, there are so many places you can turn to find a solution.

I hope when you think of me, you think of the people in your own life who have hurt you so deeply and that you find a way to forgive those people, because you just never know. Given the same circumstances that they've endured, you might possibly have turned out to be the same kind of person.

I hope I inspire you to consider that our lives are a part of a much bigger picture. Doesn't your own family display this? Your family was a part of something before you were born, and after you die, those in your family will be part of something, too!

I hope if given the chance, you love those who don't love you back. Practice has shown me that loving the unlovable is better than revenge. It's rewarding and, man, can it grow incredible flowers.

I hope you know what you believe and why you believe it!

If you've lost faith, I hope I inspire you to try one more time to believe that GOD loves you!

I hope you know that no matter who you are, I think you are awesome, valuable and unique!

I hope I inspire you to live and not waste a single moment… In joy and in pain, it's my passion to inspire you to "Find Life On The Other Side." When you learn to love and forgive yourself, it is then you can love your neighbor. It is my life's mission to spread this message like it's wildfire. ... I believe that despite our environments, we can still exercise our greatest strength and power, which are our choices. If you have made a million poor choices, start right now and make ONE good one.

The Fury of life touches us all...

Here's to all of you brave souls who live when you want to die, who give even when it hurts to give, who see past the color of our skin and past the stain of regret and see human.

To those who find a way back to life after being numb and to those who work hard every day to teach our future generations, offer wisdom, kindness and courage.

To those of you still reading this...

YOU are the bravest of souls. Never forget that!

Reflections:

As I said at the beginning of this book, depression, anxiety, and suicide doesn't discriminate. It has touched us all. I hope that somehow if you have seen yourself in this story, no matter in what chapter or on what page, you know and believe that YOUR life matters. It doesn't matter to me if you are rich or poor, a hero or villain, educated or not.

I'm not better than any one of you—not even the man who killed my husband and daughter. I came into this world with no material assets, and that is how I will leave. But I have value, my soul; all of me has value beyond riches that you or I can ever comprehend. So do you.

When it comes to being honest about your situation, whatever you do, don't lie to yourself about what's going on inside of you. At the very least, start the conversation with yourself about why you haven't gone for help. Ask yourself, what is something I can do to take control of my life?

Questions:

If you have a plan to end your life, is there anything that I can say to make you change your mind? What would that be? What do you need to hear that would help you consider making a different choice? What needs to change in your life for you to decide that it's worth being here? HOLD ON TO THIS- Never Give Up!!!

_____

_____

_____

So, who are you, really? Are you connected to your deepest purpose?

_____

_____

_____

Don't Give Up on YOU…………

"Dare You To Move" Program Launch on August 11th 2014
(Ten years after Brian and Brittany were killed)
Both McKayla and Amber were speakers at this event.

A big thank you to Megan Salazar for her remarkable
artistic work which so beautifully reminds us of how
we can rise from the ashes and find beauty in the pain.

Me and my oldest daughter McKayla

Me and my youngest daughter Amber

Proud Momma Moments

I'm so proud of these two beautiful women-
I'm honored to call them my daughters!

Chapter Seventeen

HOME

For as far back as I can remember, I have dreamed of being a mom with a beautifully decorated home, full of love, pictures, children, and memories. With all the twists and turns of my life, the meaning of HOME has taken my once idealistic view of it, shred it, and required a deeper understanding of what the word "home" means to me.

As a young mom, home was the place where my deepest heart desired that my children would grow up in a loving family and that "home" would be the place they returned to; The unmoving foundation. For years, I think I was able to create that place. However, despite my best intentions, after my long battle with depression and suicidal ideation, our home's foundation began to crack.

As I shared previously, just a few short years after this battle, in 2004, my late husband Brian and daughter were killed. When this happened, most all of our belongings were in a Uhaul truck. With no home to call our own, it was painful to piece our lives together one box at a time.

There is a song with lyrics that goes like this: "If home is where my heart is, then I'm out of place." From the moment my daughter died, my heart and soul began to grapple with the fact that a part of me now longed to be in a place where there is no more death, suffering or pain. I call this place Heaven. I imagine that my sweet daughter Brittany who struggled to walk because of her Cerebral Palsy is free today, running with the angels on streets of gold.

However, this desire to be at "home" with her chafes against the truth that I am still here, alive and very much wanting to have a place that not only I can call home, but where my other daughters, McKayla and Amber, can also call home. A place that as they build their own lives and families, they grow found of visiting.

It's been 17 years now since Brian and Brittany have physically shared a home here with us. Since that day, I wish I could tell you that early on, I was able to buy a home, settle down, and provide that physical stability for the girls. But that's just not the truth. It hurts me deeply even writing this. As I think about the promise I made as a young woman to protect my children from the pain of divorce and trauma, it's hard to look at the past. Though painful, I refuse to let it rob me of the time I do have here with them. There are dark moments when the pain likes to creep in and whisper; you've failed your daughters. There is nothing that would hurt me more than to think that I failed them. My enemy knows that a loud, disruptive voice has no place in my mind. I will not tolerate that. This haunting whisper is not talking about the ways I have let them down. I have accepted what I can't change. Instead, it speaks right to my deepest wound and fear—that I'm "unfit." That there is something wrong with me. Often, when I have days of sheer happiness, this haunting whisper says, who does that? Who carries on as if nothing has happened?

In these moments of pain, I must remind myself that I fought a battle decades ago that almost cost me my life. That battle taught me that **"It is better to be—than not to be at all." In those moments, I have to remind that haunting whisper how far I've come, reflect on every lesson I've learned and boldly say that I've only failed when I give up.** Post Traumatic Stress is a beast. It's complex and tough to navigate. If this is a battle you face, I can't think of anything more powerful than showing yourself compassion. There are so many mean people in the world, don't be mean to yourself. Make the brave decision today that you will challenge yourself to grow for the rest of your life but know you must always do it through the lens of compassion and acceptance.

Sometimes, I want to scream- "This is not what I wanted; this chaos and struggle to survive is not what I wanted." As much as I want to yell and say how unfair it is, point fingers at those who have taken so much; I find a strange sense of peace knowing that all of this pain, the moving, the loss of belongings, the instability forced me to really question, what does "home" truly mean to me.

After my brain surgery in 2012 I was left with permanent nerve damage called "Occipital Neuralgia." To treat this and maintain my pain levels I was having what are called "nerve burns," or "Radio-frequency Nerve Ablation" done. Every six months, I would have 8 of my nerves cauterized to help relieve the daily pain I faced. Having traveled across the country for speaking events, I noticed that in areas with lower altitude and less drastic barometric pressure changes, I would wake up pain free. To maintain some level of a healthy life in Colorado it required regular medical intervention.

I'll never forget this day. In 2018, I asked both of my daughters, who at the time were 20 and 24 to meet me at Dazbog, my favorite coffee shop in Loveland Co. Northern Colorado had been our home since 2006. Almost trembling, I asked them both if I had their blessing to move to Florida by myself and start over in a place where I could wake up pain free every day. The haunting whisper tells me how selfish I am for this. My heart wrestles with all of this as I begin to realize that maybe home is no longer a place, or a physical structure, but possibly the feeling of being at home with someone.

Home is where my children are. Home is wherever I am when I am with them. Home is where Brittany is at. Home is where my Creator is. Home is finding peace within myself. Home is the grand feeling of being with someone without any need to pretend, hide, fear or hold back; To find people like this is a blessing especially on this side of trauma and grief.

I've never fought in a war for our country, ran into a burning building on fire with my crew, or had to face an armed man pointing a gun at me, but I can only imagine the intense sense of belonging that must happen in these moments.

When I began the transition off of disability and re-entered the workforce in 2014, I felt like an outsider. After years of working with our First Responders, Veterans, and those who love and support them, I'm very aware of the painful transition back into civilian life. So often, they feel out of place. It is such an honor to earn the trust of those I speak and work with and enter into that sacred place where our LIES Live. The lies that tell us we are a burden. The lies that tell us that things will never get better. The lies that say, we are "unfit" and awful. On a soul level, I think they, too, understand the feeling of being at "home" with someone. Someone who sees both your strength and weakness and calls you brother or sister. Someone who is connected with you on a deeper level for a higher purpose. Over the years, my heart has found a "home" as I've connected with my audience and those I work closely with as a coach.

Personally, I feel the church has done an awful job of making people feel at home. This is heartbreaking to me. I swear there is a sign on the outside of many churches that says: "make sure you are all clean before you enter this building." I've seen many say, "all are welcome," but the moment you show symptoms of addiction or trauma, they yell "unclean." If you've ever felt this pain, I'm so sorry. In fairness, this isn't a blanket condemnation. There are many churches out there that are welcoming and non-judgmental, but the trend seems to be going in the wrong direction. I think so many want to provide real solutions regarding PTSD, suicide, and trauma but don't know where to turn.

Sadly, most marriages today never reach a place of trust where both people feel safe and at home with their partners.

If life hasn't turned out the way that you had dreamed of… if what you see in the mirror is not what you thought it would be… if the desire to have more and be more has not satisfied your soul, then maybe you too can understand the feeling of being out of place in this world. How can this place be "home" when death is still a reality? Until I see my sweet Brittany again, I know that a part of my soul will always long to be home with her.

And yet-

Almost six years ago, on my way up to release balloons at Brian and Brittany's graveside, I stopped to grab the balloons in King Soopers as usual. As the lady behind the counter turned to grab the balloons, I noticed a card, and it said, "Keep Laugh On Your To-Do List." I felt this spiritual beckon and I swear it was as if my daughter Brittany was saying, "Mom, it's ok to be whole. I'm good. While you are alive, Live! Don't waste a single minute." I made a promise to her that day that I would "Add Laughter" to the top of my to-do list. I wasn't sure how, but nonetheless, I still made the promise.

Joy and laughter were some of the most challenging treasures for me to find on this side of grief. I have worked very hard to keep that promise. Absolute joy is hard to find on the other side of burying a child. It took me some time to sort through why. What I've come to realize is that any time I would step into the river of Joy and Life with both feet—I felt like I was leaving Brittany behind, so I would quickly plant one foot back down in the river of grief where she was. Now that I understand how guilt and grief work, I've been able to stand with both feet in the river of Joy and Life and know, that she is right there walking with me. I've not left her behind. It's ok to walk in this river and carry both the pain and joy. Understanding this has allowed me to open my heart to being at "Home" right here, in the here and now. Living in Florida near the ocean has brought such joy to my life.

When I first moved to Florida three years ago, I didn't get on dating websites. I didn't put myself out there. For the first time in my life, I was totally ok being just me. You may not understand the magnitude of growth that had to happen for me to spend a day, alone at the beach, but I do. One day after spending an entire day by myself at the beach I stopped in Island Time to watch a football game. My car pulled up at the exact moment as the man who now holds my heart in the palm of his hands.

Somehow while wrestling with life, death, grief, and new beginnings… I found a human who has created such a beautiful space and trust in our relationship that I can now say, "My home is with you. My soul has found the one whom I love."

I still find it funny how we met. It's actual rom-com material. We arrived at the same time. Jeremy would later reveal that he strategically chose a spot where he thought the pretty lady who arrived simultaneously would sit. I sat across the bar instead as I wanted to have a good view of the football game. Undeterred, he came over about 30 minutes later and politely introduced himself. Upon discovering that I was new in town, he gave me his business card and told me to call if I needed advice from a local. And then he LEFT. Who does that?

Little did Jeremy know at the time how much I absolutely loved his no-strings, respectful, put the ball in my court approach. It worked so well that I called him a day or two later. He was out clothes shopping. What man does this, let alone admits to it. We hit it off right away, given our mutual interests, particularly in music. On the night of our first date, we randomly ran into one of the men who was there at Island Time the night we first met, and he appallingly exclaimed, "you're with business card guy?" We both still laugh at that one. Fittingly, it says right on his business card that he is a Relationship Manager. His friends even give him a hard time hearing this story, but a few of them have openly pondered whether or not to try this approach.

It took me 40 plus years of growth, survival and failure to finally meet someone who sees all of me, loves me for me, cheers on my success, and is not quick to be angry or jealous. I found a man that is funny, loved and respected by many. A man who is clear on what matters to him, who has tasted just enough defeat, regret and loss to know that life is much more about love than it is ego.

For the first time ever, I found someone to fight fair with; Someone who knows the power in compromise. By this time in my life, I've had so many failed relationships, I wasn't sure that healthy relationships even existed on this side of loss, grief, and PTSD. Boy, did I ever test Jeremy. His first test was my youngest daughter Amber. It turns out she is a pretty good judge of character.

From the night we first met, it was apparent to both Jeremy and me that we shared an incredible passion for music. On our first date, after a lovely dinner and fun evening shooting pool, we did some car-aoke and were singing songs together on the drive home. I felt like a lovestruck teenager. A few months into our relationship, he asked if I would like to come over for dinner, and I thought, sure, let's see what you got! The man can cook. When he asked if it was ok if he turned on some music while he was prepping the chicken for homemade "lettuce wraps," I said, "of course," and smiled. When Frank Sinatra came on, tears started rolling down my face. Music has this transcending way to connect me with those I love. Instantly, I thought of my dad, Carol, and my grandparents.

Some of my favorite moments over the last three years are the two of us singing karaoke. After a day of work, we'd take off, catch a sunset and then you'd find us doing our favorite duet- Bring Me To Life by Evanescence. Without fail, I nearly always sing "Hold On" by Wilson Phillips and think of my mom and brother Jeff.

I knew I had found someone special when Jeremy sang "One In A Million" to me at a country bar- He didn't care what people thought of him belting out an r&b love song. He simply wanted to express how much he loved me through music. By my count, we've sang karaoke in over 33 spots spanning many great cities and states. Like clockwork, whether he is with me for an event or I tag along with him to one of his, we always try to find a spot to sing. To date, our list includes Nashville, Seattle, Denver, LA, Pittsburgh, Branson, Boston, New York, Sarasota, Des Moines, Dallas, New Orleans, Atlanta, Tucson, Tallahassee and Portland. I'm looking forward to crossing many more places off our list as there is no one I'd rather go through life with than him. We're each other's shotgun rider.

In 2020, Jeremy and I started the year off with his birthday in Puerto Rico. Keeping my promise to Brittany to add laughter to the top of my to-do list, I convinced Jeremey to go zip lining. Next time, he said he'd gladly cheer me on from the sidelines, but zip lining was not for him.

In early February, we got to visit Jeremy's mom, Roberta, for the last time before she passed away. She had been sick for quite some time, in and out of the hospital. On one of our trips up, I asked her if she would like her nails painted. She was so thrilled that I offered to do that. So, on our next visit, I painted her nails a light pink color. As her health declined, you could hear the resolve in her voice. You could tell she was ready to go home as she had lost her twin brother, Robert, the year before and Jeremy's dad, Don, 20 years prior. When we were standing in the hospital room in February, I knew it would be the last time I would see her. I asked her if she wanted to pray. We had not talked much about Faith or God, so it took some courage for me to ask her. She smiled and said she would love that. We all held hands as I said the Lord's Prayer. It was this same prayer that David, my step-dad and I prayed as we stood with my mom when she died. I gave Roberta a long hug and kissed her on her forehead. I couldn't say it out loud—but I was thinking, please, when you get "Home" and see my mom and Brittany, will you hug and kiss them for me. I cried the entire way home. That was the last time we saw Jeremy's mom.

We had already made plans to fly out to Colorado to see Amber for her birthday. Jeremy conspired with Amber to pull off a night of karaoke with McKayla. I was thrilled to spend the night together. We ate food at Amber's place then we took an uber ride into town. Watching both of my girls sing just for the fun of it was a blast. In those simple moments,

I take in all that we have been through and thank God that I'm alive. Leaving them is always hard for me to do. How can I not possibly fear losing them? I know that my ability to wrap this fear up and tuck it away is a learned practice. I honor the fear and keep moving.

We finished that month strong in Pennsylvania. It was such an honor to be the keynote speaker at the Wounded Warrior Patrol Annual Event. I've been speaking for a long time, but this event was unique for me. This was the first time I spoke to both the Veterans and family members in attendance.

We had no idea that a global pandemic was about to happen. Life for everyone came to a halt, and most people were forced to pivot. Travel stopped, and for months both Jeremy and I worked from home, rarely leaving.

When Amber found out that she would be forced to work from home, she caught a flight out to Florida. For almost three months, Amber stayed with us as she was able to work remotely during all of this. Amber and I settled into a routine of walking around the lake every morning, and making coffee became something to look forward to. Our two-bedroom apartment turned into a three-person office suite. We would all peek out of our corners and let the others know who needed to be quiet for calls coming up. Even though I had the "office" with closed doors, I could still hear the two of them. It was hilarious. With the beaches barricaded due to Covid it was tough to be in Florida together and not be able to enjoy to beach.

Though stressful, Jeremy and I decided that because our lease was up and we didn't want to rent for another year, we wanted to buy a house by year's end. We had no idea that we would find our dream home in Tallahassee. Coincidentally, Tallahassee is Jeremy's old stomping grounds, as this is where he obtained his undergraduate degree. We successfully jumped through all of the hoops of buying a home, and the closing date was in sight.

Weeks before closing on the house, my sister messaged me and said-Shuane's gone. Our brother had been in the midst of his own battle with PTSD and mental warfare, and sadly, he lost that battle. I was utterly side-swiped. I had no idea. I remember telling Jeremy; this will take me a while to get through. I distinctly recall saying, "I will probably enter in the Dark Maze of depression." I reassured him that I wasn't suicidal or anything like that, but I was in a deep place of pain and grief. I promised him that I knew how to get out of the Dark Maze; I would just need time. I cried for weeks, almost non-stop. For me, everything in my life, except for my coaching clients, came to a halt. I struggled with what the proper reaction was to all of this, in regard to work and business endeavors, including this book. I wondered, should I cancel my client sessions? Should I put on my brave face and not say anything? Should I let them know the pain I was in and say, "I'm still here to walk alongside you, just know, I'm grieving?" I chose the latter, and every one of my clients thanked me for my honesty and for how I showed up so authentically. As you can imagine, this was an awful lot to deal with for my entire family and us.

No relationship is perfect, just as no one among us is perfect. For my part, I work hard every day to manage my symptoms of PTSD. Going through all of this caused some major triggers for me. When that happens between us, I can see the look of confusion on Jeremy's face. He gets this childlike look of "yikes, what did I do?" I rely heavily on communication at this point on my journey and typically express what is happening and apologize if needed. As I recall other relationships in my life while facing so much pressure, grief, and pain, I've yet to have a loving partner who was as caring, constant and funny as Jeremy. Together we successfully navigated these significant life changes during all of this chaos, loss, and disruption in our world. I can count on one hand the times where significant conflicts flared up over this last year. It is in the way that we always work through these things that allow my heart to trust him more and fall more in love with him.

I welcome the day when travel opens back up so we can add more locations and memories to our list where we have sung karaoke together.

With our roots firmly planted in Tallahassee, it brings me great joy to think of our future and the hope of memories created near and far with our children, friends, family and loved ones.... and as I hold close to my heart those whom we love who have gone on ahead of us I realize that, for me, HOME is no longer a place or structure; rather, it is where those I love are. And in some incredible way- that means that my "home" is far-reaching - a free and wild thing...

Gone Too Soon

I dedicate this section to my younger brother SSG Shuane Patrick Moore 2-35 Infantry, who lost his battle with PTSD on September 11th, 2020. Shaune served two tours, one in Iraq and Afghanistan.

I've struggled to write this dedication and have sat on moving forward with this book, maybe for lack of words to say. Possibly, writing this and finally sharing it has some finality that I don't want to face.

10.24.1981 - 9.11.2020

When my husband and daughter died, my brother, Shaune, took leave and came home for their service. During the service, Shaune was one of Brittany's pallbearers. Shaune's son was the joy of his life. Shaune, I will never know how long you had been fighting such darkness and pain or the depth of the battle you faced. We can only piece together what was happening in your life as we sort through your final days. We miss you; you are a good man. Shuane, thank you for your service and sacrifice. I'm sorry I let you down brother! I love you.

I'd like to take a moment and say how incredibly proud I am of my sister Kim and step-mom Carol. Due to the global pandemic, they had to deal with the aftermath of this— just the two of them— in Alaska over a short three-day period. You both have the spirit of WARRIORS. I love you both.

Shaune with McKayla and his son Eli

Gone Too Soon-

Sadly, all I know is that as a family we are now a part of the national and global crisis of losing over 22 service members a day. I cannot help but feel the pain of "what if?" Would you still be here if you had read my book, Doc Springer's book WARRIOR, or been folded into our joint mission to provide real solutions to the real problems our nation's Warriors are facing?

As I conclude writing this book, it is with the heaviest of hearts that I share the story behind the story of "Redefine Your Mission."

I met Doc Springer early in 2020, right before Covid became a global pandemic. We had a mutual connection on LinkedIn, Andrew Holycross, a warrior who served in the military, who saw my posts, story, mission and work. He messaged both of us and told us he was going to connect us. To me, he said, "the two of you really should talk" and to Doc Springer, he said, "my gut is telling me that I need to connect you and Jennifer Tracy."

I'll never forget the first time we talked. I remember this sigh as we began the conversation, and the moment of silence before we dove in. I could tell that Shauna was a busy woman. We both had no idea why Andrew wanted us to connect. But he was insistent, and both of us know that people like Andrew, who are wired as warriors, often have very great instincts.

So I do what I typically do in this kind of silent moment- I share a little bit about who I am and why I do the work I do. I remember her saying, "ahhhh, I think I totally understand now why Andrew wanted us to connect."

Doc Springer is an incredible listener. She had soaked up every last word I had said. Then it happened. She said, "I'm equally passionate about the things that you are Jennifer. Can I share a blog I wrote about this very topic?"

As I read it, I had this very strange feeling. Her perspective, her views on how to truly come alongside the suffering, her tenacious spirit to fight for what is right and just, came through in all of her work. I said, "Shauna, can I send you my book? So much of what you are saying is what I wrote about three years ago in my book, *Inside 'The Mind' of Suicide.*"

So, we traded our books written long before Andrew ever connected us. She sent me her first book, *Marriage, For Equals,* and her latest book, WARRIOR*: How to Support Those Who Protect Us* and I sent her mine. Again, I was astounded at how aligned we were.

Now don't mistake me here. If you read her book and mine, you will see that she is much more eloquent with her words. My youngest daughter Amber says that I write like I talk. As I read Shauna's words though, what became very clear was that we had both come to some very powerful conclusions. Doc Springer later told me that in that first conversation with me, she instinctively recognized me as a "sister in arms" in the same battle that she has also been driven to take head on.

In fact, as our collaboration developed over time, when she first showed her husband (also a psychologist) a picture of me, he said, "that's interesting. I wouldn't say that you look the same, but there is something in your faces that is similar - maybe it's that you both have a strong jawline or something similar in your eyes - the best way to describe it is that her eyes also show a mix of strength and compassion."

To reach those struggling with a mental health battle, you have to be able to understand the enemy inside the mind. You have to bring it to life, and help those suffering see the unseen. You have to build trust within the Tribe to effectively create change.

Initial conversations led to months of late night work on a project called "Redefine Your Mission." Our mission is to compile the most important lessons we have learned about winning mental health battles, and to package them in an affordable, practical way. Mid-way through, I had mentioned to Shauna that I really wanted to put out a version 2.0 of my book. I had additional lessons to add and I wanted to change up the title and cover. I'm thankful that, like me, she was very supportive of my passion. She was willing to wait for me to make these updates before the launch of our initiative.

Tears are streaming down my face as I think about my brother Shaune and his son. How can I not help but wonder... if I had just moved along as planned would my brother still be here?

Now don't get me wrong. I've been here before. I have not buried a husband and child and navigated a nearly lethal battle with suicidal ideation and PTSD by giving in to guilt and shame. I came out on the other side of that battle, and I know that there is HOPE.

However, the truth is, I will never know if our joint efforts would have helped Shaune. What I can do is take the pain of that loss and use it as fuel for the continual mission of supporting those who are struggling with mental health battles.

How is it that you and I are given such freedom at the expense of our nations warriors and first responders, and all the while they are suffering?

One of my favorite quotes is, "In The Pursuit of Saving Lives… Don't Forget To Save Your Own." When you're a Warrior, First Responder or leader, you are trained to put others above yourself.

It is very hard to convince someone with this mindset that "suffering silently" **is not a noble part of your calling as a warrior.**

If a real enemy is coming against you- it's noble to lay down your life and fight. If your brother or sister is wounded and you lay down your life fighting to save them, that is noble.

You would never think of going into enemy territory without your team or your unit, and a well developed strategy for that battle. Or for that matter, think about someone you love. Would you want them to fight a mental health battle alone and isolated? Why would you think that fighting a mental health battle is any different? Stop believing the lie that you are meant to fight these types of battles alone.

If you love, support, or serve alongside those who protect us, please be kind to yourself if you feel that you have let them down by not knowing how to support them. So many of us have.

One of my favorite testimonials about WARRIOR and Doc Springer's work is this statement, made by Sgt. Eddie Wright:

[Doc Springer] calls to our strength and she walks with us in a way that translates like this: I see the challenges before you, and I can help you get clear on them as well. Now, get up and fight.

Sgt. Eddie Wright, USMC (Ret), Bravo Co. 2nd Plt. 1st Recon. Bn. OIF I, II

It is in this spirit that we launch our collaborative efforts to support those who make continual sacrifices for all of us. We see you, and you *matter* to us.

www.redefineyourmission.com

Afterthoughts & Resources

Suicide Danger with Social Media

When I had my battle with suicide 20 years ago, the only people who knew about it were the people closest to me and those I wanted or needed to share it with. After being in the psychiatric unit, my life did not quickly turn around. It was most definitely a process- a lot of "two steps forward and one step back." As I have already shared, the guilt and shame I felt when I first was admitted into the psychiatric unit was intense, but as time went on, the pain and grief began to lift.

Today on social media, I have worked hard to present the truest version of myself. I tend to be pretty honest about the things I have faced in my life. With that said, there have been times where people have intentionally communicated false things about me and have used social media to attack my character.

I can think of three times in the last six years when things were said and spread about me that were not true. I had people reach out to me privately and ask what was going on, but there were many who didn't. I've wondered, what do those people think who don't know the truth? Sometimes I run into people and have found myself feeling nervous and anxious around them. It's the unknowing that bothers me; it's not actually the confrontation or even the negativity. The reason I'm sharing this in a book about suicide is because I believe social media can have a negative effect on those who are struggling.

Several people put their best face forward on social media. They truly are happy, busy, enjoying every moment with friends and family, while some people put on a front and hide behind it. My own personal struggle with grief has, at times, made it hard to find a balance on social media. Have you ever experienced the social world where you can get your feelings hurt by how many likes you get on a post or photo? When you are struggling with anxiety, depression or thoughts of suicide, the social media world can be hard to navigate. Have you ever wondered why people that used to like your photos don't anymore? It's possible they didn't see your post, but the not knowing can be hard. It's unseen. If something like this happened only once, it might not be a big deal, but if someone to your face acts like they are your friend, yet likes and comments on everyone else's post and not yours, that can be hurtful. That is a form of social passive/aggressive behavior. It can mess with you. I can only speak from my experience; this type of behavior can hurt just as much as a punch in the gut.

To understand this type of behavior, let me define for you what passive/aggressive means: It is a type of behavior or personality characterized by an avoidance of direct confrontation. Instead of someone having the courage to tell you how they feel, they take out their anger on you or others with non verbal aggressive behavior.

For people who don't think about things like this, how many times have we seen someone post something about an accident or the death of a loved one? We typically respond to those things. For someone who is struggling, creating drama may be their way of trying to reach out, sometimes unknowingly even to themselves.

There is also the obvious part of social media where people choose to say mean and hateful things while they hide behind their cell phones and computers, but would never have the courage to say what they say or have a face-to-face conversation with someone in person about how they feel.

In the end, to me the most important thing to do regarding social media is to talk about how you feel with real people. If you are a parent of a child who is struggling, bring this up and honor how the entire social media world can be hard to navigate, especially for someone who is struggling. Make a connection with someone who you know genuinely cares about you outside of social media. Possibly take some time off from social media all together.

Like I said before, fight for you! Don't let people mistreat you. There are so many people that care and will listen.

Afterthoughts on Condemnation

I have been asked: Do you think people who die by suicide are condemned by God? This is a tough question to answer.

A lot of people who lose loved ones to suicide struggle with guilt and fear that because their loved ones took their own lives, God will condemn them. If you have lost someone that you love to suicide, I'm sorry for your loss. I've felt the deep heavy weight of loss, and I know how painful that is. I, too, have lost loved ones to suicide. It's confusing.

On the other side of suicide, I can open my heart and share with you that when I was depressed and suicidal, my mind was not working properly—just like someone who is diagnosed with diabetes requires insulin to stay alive and knows that if it's withheld, it can be life-threatening. Likewise, lacking proper amounts of serotonin can be life-threatening for someone who is depressed or having suicidal thoughts. Lack of proper sleep and low serotonin levels caused me to have dangerous, sicking thoughts.

I know that this is a tough subject. There have been many horrific events where people have done very disturbing acts, murdering others and then themselves. While it is hard to comprehend, and like I said before, I felt like my mind had been kidnapped and held for ransom.

I don't believe that we are judged by the last act that we did here on earth.

Suicide Awareness

THINGS YOU CAN DO

Prevention-

Simply stated- Suicide Prevention can be an innovative way to solve this complex issue. Communication and taking an active approach can help prevent more serious issues from occurring.

Intervention-

This time frame is categorized as someone who already has symptoms of depression, thoughts of suicide, hopelessness or suicidal ideation. The ASIST program does an incredible job of helping every day men and women learn how to intervene confidently in times of crisis. I wish every one had this training.

Postvention-

What is Postvention? Postvention is a term often used in the suicide prevention field. The definition below is from the U.S. national guidelines developed by the Survivors of Suicide Loss Task Force.1 [Postvention is] an organized response in the aftermath of a suicide to accomplish any one or more of the following: To facilitate the healing of individuals from the grief and distress of suicide loss To mitigate other negative effects of exposure to suicide To prevent suicide among people who are at high risk after exposure to suicide.

Reference 1. Survivors of Suicide Loss Task Force. (2015, April). Responding to grief, trauma, and distress after a suicide: U.S. National Guidelines (p. 1). Washington, DC: National Action Alliance for Suicide Prevention. Retrieved from http://www.sprc.org/resources-programs/responding-grief-trauma-and-distress-after-suicide-usnational-guidelines [6]

RESOURCES FOR SUICIDE
NATIONAL SUICIDE PREVENTION LIFELINE
Call 1-800-273-8255
Available 24 Hours Everyday

Fire/EMS Helpline: 1-888-731-FIRE (3473)

COPLINE: 1-800-267-5463 operational
24 hours a day / 7 days a week Calls are answered by peers. All calls and emails are strictly 100% CONFIDENTIAL.

Veterans Crisis Line: 1-800-273-8255
Confidential- Available every day, 24/7.

K-Love Radio-Positive encouraging music. People to pray with you. K-love is a national radio station. Website www.klove.com

FOR MORE RESOURCES

ONLINE ACCESS

VIDEOS

BOOK GUIDE

FREE ADDITIONAL WORKSHEETS

WWW.JENNIFERTRACY-INSPIRE.COM/BOOKS

YOUR

WORKSHEETS
& JOURNAL

*Making
The Pieces
Fit*

While you are alive...
Live

Jennifer Tracy

START HERE

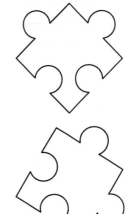

Win Your Battle

Putting it together one piece at a time. Making it through will require you to give attention to the multiple pieces.

Your diagnosis does not define you--

It highlights what you must overcome if you want your life back.

Your thoughts don't define you.

Your inadequacies don't define you.

Your past does not define you.

What defines you are the actions you take every day to be a person of excellence.

Excellence must not be mistaken for perfection. Knowing this is essential if you are fighting to overcome anxiety, grief, depression, or PTSD.

You must love who you are right now and work on yourself each day because you know your worth.

When you are struggling and you show up for practice, that matters.

Jennifer Tracy

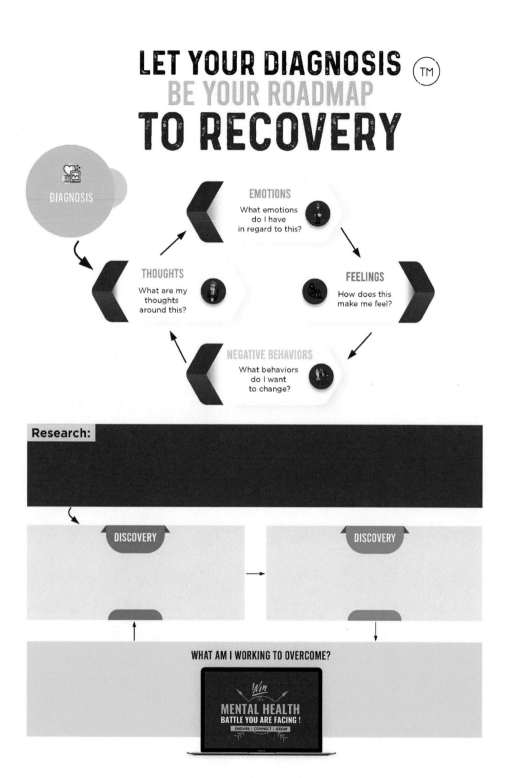

LET YOUR DIAGNOSIS (TM)
BE YOUR ROADMAP
TO RECOVERY

DIAGNOSIS

EMOTIONS
What emotions do I have in regard to this?

THOUGHTS
What are my thoughts around this?

FEELINGS
How does this make me feel?

NEGATIVE BEHAVIORS
What behaviors do I want to change?

Research:

DISCOVERY

DISCOVERY

WHAT AM I WORKING TO OVERCOME?

Win the
MENTAL HEALTH
BATTLE YOU ARE FACING !
ENDURE | CONNECT | GROW

Jennifer Tracy Inspire, LLC ~Redefine Your Mission (TM)

LET YOUR DIAGNOSIS
BE YOUR ROADMAP
TO RECOVERY ™

DIAGNOSIS

EMOTIONS
What emotions do I have in regard to this?

THOUGHTS
What are my thoughts around this?

FEELINGS
How does this make me feel?

NEGATIVE BEHAVIORS
What behaviors do I want to change?

WHAT ARE YOU FACING

Jennifer Tracy Inspire, LLC ~Redefine Your Mission ™

RESEARCH YOUR BARRIERS

So often we worry about the stigma associated with the battles we are facing. What I want you to do is pretend that someone you love needs your help. Research the topic that you are dealing with. Learn all you can about it.

WHAT DO YOU WANT TO OVERCOME?

WHAT DO YOU ALREADY KNOW ABOUT IT?

WHAT ARE YOUR FEELINGS ABOUT THIS?

Before we begin, it is crucial that you get clear on where you are at today! Take some time to rate each of these areas in your life.

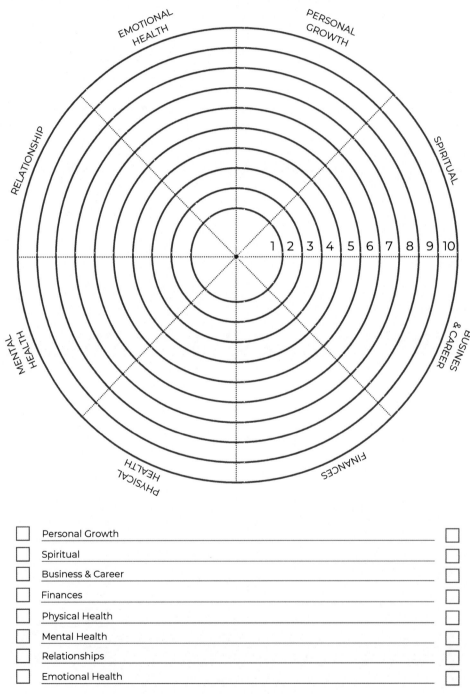

☐	Personal Growth	☐
☐	Spiritual	☐
☐	Business & Career	☐
☐	Finances	☐
☐	Physical Health	☐
☐	Mental Health	☐
☐	Relationships	☐
☐	Emotional Health	☐

Jennifer Tracy Inspire, LLC ~Redefine Your Mission

BREAK IT-DOWN
PERSONAL GROWTH

Instructions:

Write out everything in the area of personal growth in your life right now that you want to pay attention to. Highlight or circle things on this list that others can help you with.

1. _____
2. _____
3. _____
4. _____
5. _____
6. _____
7. _____
8. _____
9. _____
10. _____

Next Step:
Do this for each step in the circle.

BREAK IT-DOWN
MENTAL HEALTH

Instructions:

Write out everything in the area of mental health in your life right now that you want to pay attention to. Highlight or circle things on this list that others can help you with.

1. _____

2. _____

3. _____

4. _____

5. _____

6. _____

7. _____

8. _____

9. _____

10. _____

Next Step:

Do this for each step in the circle.

BREAK IT-DOWN
SPIRITUAL

Instructions:

Write out everything spiritually happening in your life right now that you want to pay attention to. Highlight or circle things on this list that others can help you with.

1. _____
2. _____
3. _____
4. _____
5. _____
6. _____
7. _____
8. _____
9. _____
10. _____

Next Step:

Do this for each step in the circle.

BREAK IT-DOWN
BUSINESS & CAREER

Instructions:

Write out everything in the area of your career or business right now that you want to pay attention to. Highlight or circle things on this list that others can help you with.

1. _____
2. _____
3. _____
4. _____
5. _____
6. _____
7. _____
8. _____
9. _____
10. _____

Next Step:

Do this for each step in the circle.

BREAK IT-DOWN
FINANCIALLY

Instructions:

Write out everything in the area of your finances right now that you want to pay attention to. Highlight or circle things on this list that others can help you with.

1. _____

2. _____

3. _____

4. _____

5. _____

6. _____

7. _____

8. _____

9. _____

10. _____

Next Step:

Do this for each step in the circle.

BREAK IT-DOWN
PHYSICAL HEALTH

Instructions:

Write out everything in the area of your physical health right now that you want to pay attention to. Highlight or circle things on this list that others can help you with.

1. _____
2. _____
3. _____
4. _____
5. _____
6. _____
7. _____
8. _____
9. _____
10. _____

Next Step:

Do this for each step in the circle.

BREAK IT-DOWN
RELATIONSHIPS

Instructions:

Write out everything going on in the area of the relationships right now that you want to pay attention to. Highlight or circle things on this list that you want to address

1. _____

2. _____

3. _____

4. _____

5. _____

6. _____

7. _____

8. _____

9. _____

10. _____

Next Step:
Do this for each step in the circle.

BREAK IT-DOWN
EMOTIONAL

Instructions:

Write out everything emotionally happening in your life right now that you want to pay attention to. Highlight or circle things on this list that others can help you with.

1. _____

2. _____

3. _____

4. _____

5. _____

6. _____

7. _____

8. _____

9. _____

10. _____

Next Step:

Do this for each step in the circle.

RESET YOUR INTENTIONS

Before we begin, it is crucial that you get clear on what you want in each area of your life to look like instead. Take some time to fill in the spaces below.

PERSONAL GROWTH	PHYSICAL HEALTH

SPIRITUAL	MENTAL HEALTH

BUSINESS	CAREER	RELATIONSHIPS

FINANCES	EMOTIONAL HEALTH

CHART YOUR GROWTH

As you go through each chapter- write the page number where you learn something new in each category.

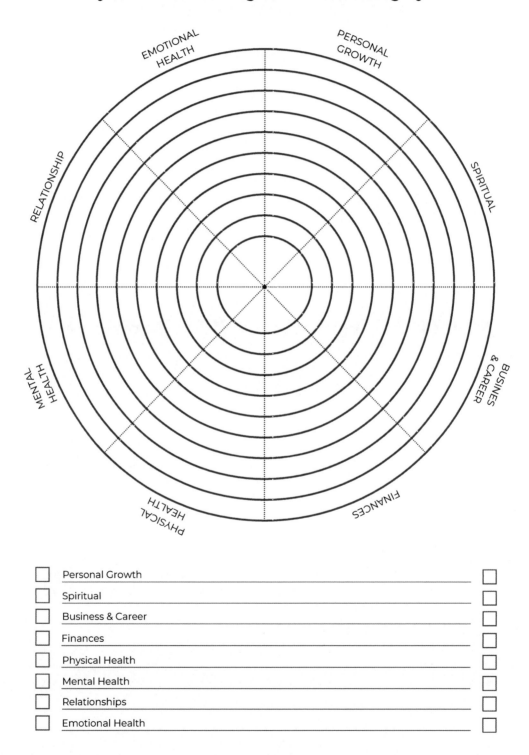

☐	Personal Growth	☐
☐	Spiritual	☐
☐	Business & Career	☐
☐	Finances	☐
☐	Physical Health	☐
☐	Mental Health	☐
☐	Relationships	☐
☐	Emotional Health	☐

What are some barriers you face that stand in the way of your growth? Research these.

KNOW YOUR BARRIERS

VICTIM
MENTALITY

FINANCIAL
RESOURCES

LACK OF
SUPPORT

LOSS OF
PURPOSE

BLACK &
WHITE
THINKING

LOW SELF
WORTH

PHYSICAL
LIMITATIONS

BLACK & WHITE THINKING

CHANGE EVERYTHING INTO A POSITIVE I STATEMENT

Here are some examples of black & white thinking. Use the following sheet to think of ways this plays out in your life.

NEGATIVE THOUGHT:

I'm Disabled & Have PTSD

POSITIVE AFFIRMATION

I can positively manage my symptoms of PTSD

NEGATIVE THOUGHT:

I'm Fat

POSITIVE AFFIRMATION:

I have fat on my body but I am not defined by it.

NEGATIVE THOUGHT:

I'm a Failure

POSITIVE AFFIRMATION:

I have failed at many things but I choose to learn from those failures.

NEGATIVE THOUGHT:

I'm Needy

POSITIVE AFFIRMATION:

I have needs and it is okay for me to find ways to take care of them.

BLACK & WHITE THINKING

CHANGE EVERYTHING INTO A POSITIVE I STATEMENT

NEGATIVE THOUGHT: POSITIVE AFFIRMATION:

NEGATIVE THOUGHT: POSITIVE AFFIRMATION:

NEGATIVE THOUGHT: POSITIVE AFFIRMATION:

NEGATIVE THOUGHT: POSITIVE AFFIRMATION:

BARRIERS TO GROWTH

What are some barriers you face that stand in the way of your growth?

KNOW YOUR BARRIERS

TO BEGIN

TODAY"S DATE _____

How well would you rate your mental health?

(1) — (2) — (3) — (4) — (5) — (6) — (7) — (8) — (9) — (10)

Worst   Best

How would you rate your sleep?

(1) — (2) — (3) — (4) — (5) — (6) — (7) — (8) — (9) — (10)

Worst   Best

How would you rate your relationships overall?

(1) — (2) — (3) — (4) — (5) — (6) — (7) — (8) — (9) — (10)

Worst   Best

How well would you rate your emotional wellness?

(1) — (2) — (3) — (4) — (5) — (6) — (7) — (8) — (9) — (10)

Worst   Best

How well would you rate your physical wellbeing?

(1) — (2) — (3) — (4) — (5) — (6) — (7) — (8) — (9) — (10)

Worst   Best

"There is a dark side to Resilience. It can feed the need to be perfect. Resilience without proper care can be deadly, I know! Please don't struggle silently any longer..."

Jennifer Tracy

CHAPTER THOUGHTS

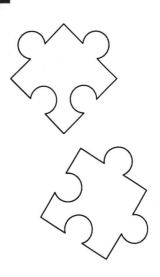

CHAPTER THOUGHTS

CHAPTER THOUGHTS

CHAPTER THOUGHTS

CHAPTER THOUGHTS

CHAPTER THOUGHTS

CHAPTER THOUGHTS

CHAPTER THOUGHTS

CHAPTER THOUGHTS

CHAPTER THOUGHTS

CHAPTER THOUGHTS

CHAPTER THOUGHTS

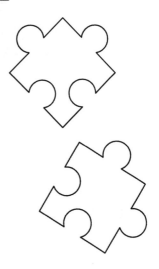

STOP COMPARISON

STOP COMPARING YOURSELF TO OTHERS

✔ I WILL MEASURE MYSELF TO MYSELF

BEFORE I FELT...   AFTER I FELT...

✔ ONE AREA I STRUGGLE-CURRENTLY

CURRENTLY I'M AT   MY GOAL...

✔ AFTER ONE MONTH-

BEFORE I FELT...   AFTER I FELT...

DEFINE YOUR WAR

Take some time to map out what your WAR is. What will it take to win this? Why is important to you?

MY WAR

Lose The Battle...
WIN The WAR

Jennifer Tracy

SELF ASSESMENTS

TO END

TODAY"S DATE _____

How well would you rate your mental health?

1	2	3	4	5	6	7	8	9	10

Worst   Best

How would you rate your sleep?

1	2	3	4	5	6	7	8	9	10

Worst   Best

How would you rate your relationships overall?

1	2	3	4	5	6	7	8	9	10

Worst   Best

How well would you rate your emotional wellness?

1	2	3	4	5	6	7	8	9	10

Worst   Best

How well would you rate your physical wellbeing?

1	2	3	4	5	6	7	8	9	10

Worst   Best

RELEASE YOUR PAST

What are you ready to release, before you begin your journey? Take some time to fill in the spaces below with all the things you are ready to release.

MY BIGGEST STRUGGLES

MY BIGGEST FEARS

RECLAIM YOUR DESIRES

It's time to reclaim your deepest desires. Fill in the spaces below with what you want to feel, what you want to accomplish and who you want to become...

HOW DO YOU WANT TO **FEEL**?

WHAT DO YOU WANT TO **ACCOMPLISH**?

WHO YOU DO WANT TO **BECOME**?

RESET YOUR INTENTIONS

Before we begin, it is crucial that you get clear on what you want each area of your life to look like instead. So take some time to fill in the spaces below.

PERSONAL GROWTH

PHYSICAL HEALTH

SPIRITUAL

MENTAL HEALTH

BUSINESS | CAREER

RELATIONSHIPS

FINANCES

EMOTIONAL HEALTH

FINAL REFLECTIONS

Complete this after you finish your journal. Fill in the space below with how you feel in your body, your mind and even your soul. Describe the emotions, thoughts and insights you have.

MY EXPERIENCE

EXTRAS

SELF-CARE CHECKLIST

WEEK OF: _____

	M	T	W	T	F	S	S

BASIC

8 hours sleep

drink water

tidy up your room/house

PHYSICAL

30 min exercize

spa day

take a different route while walking

give or receive a hug

deep and slow breathing

connect with a friend

MENTAL / EMOTIONAL

journal

digital detox

no news day

DIY, coloring, drawing

reading books

support group

ACTION PLAN

Write out tangible steps that you
want to take to reach your goals.

Instructions:

After you write all of these out, circle the top three that are of
most importance to you!

1. _____

2. _____

3. _____

4. _____

5. _____

6. _____

7. _____

8. _____

9. _____

10. _____

Love
Who You Are Becoming

○————————○

Becoming the person
you want to be
doesn't happen
overnight.

It happens by
getting up every
day and making the
CHOICE to be that person...
And...doing that every day
for the rest of your life.

Jennifer Tracy

MEET JENNIFER

Jennifer Tracy was born and raised in Colorado and resided there until 2018. She has deep roots in Northern Colorado, with many friends and family still living there, including her two exquisitely beautiful adult daughters, McKayla and Amber.

Jennifers courageous move to Florida though bittersweet brought the ocean's tranquility and freedom from the permanent pain she faced after her Chiari I Brain Malformation Decompression in 2012. The move to Florida brought about many new beginnings, including new business endeavors, a song collaboration with her daughter Amber, and meeting the love of her life, Jeremy Fleeman, in late 2018. Jennifer and Jeremy recently married and reside in Tallahassee. They share a love of music, travel, road trips, spontaneous karaoke, and cooking together.

Jennifer finds deep strength and inspiration from her faith, family, and her friends. Now that her daughters are grown, she finds herself being a bit more adventurous. She lives out her most significant purpose in two distinct ways- enjoying life on this side of grief with her daughters and family and through her business endeavors as a life coach, National Speaker, and writer. One of her all-time favorite books is Wild at Heart by John Eldredge.

 WWW.JENNIFERTRACY-INSPIRE.COM

Made in the USA
Coppell, TX
21 April 2022

76868473R00131